DESTINED TO FLY
The Pursuit of Purpose

ARIANNE MOCKABEE

WestBow
PRESS
A DIVISION OF THOMAS NELSON

Edited by: Godzchild Productions
Cover Designed by: Michelle Redmond, Custom Visual Solutions
Author photo by Michael Bailey.

WestBow Press books may be ordered through booksellers or by contacting:

WestBow Press
A Division of Thomas Nelson
1663 Liberty Drive
Bloomington, IN 47403
www.westbowpress.com
1-(866) 928-1240

ISBN: 978-1-4497-9566-5 (sc)
ISBN: 978-1-4497-9567-2 (e)

Library of Congress Control Number: 2013909260

Printed in the United States of America.

WestBow Press rev. date: 06/21/2013

films

www.thebashfilms.com

If you truly want to experience next level living with purpose, this book is a must read! Truly inspiring and full of practical insight on biblical principles that you can apply to your life and stretch your faith like never before. Exceptional!

Bianca A. Ashton
Founder & Executive Producer
B.A.S.H Films

TABLE OF CONTENTS

This book is dedicated to the memory of my Grandpap,
Cornelius A. Mockabee

I love you.

INTRODUCTION

Most of my adult life I have been trying to figure out why I'm here, what I'm supposed to be doing, and what purpose God has for me, if any. I kept to myself for the most part growing up, and had a few close friends here and there. I accepted Christ as a teen, and grew up in church not fully understanding life beyond salvation. After I graduated from high school and started college, I thought I was grown and could make it on my own, without God. I still believed in Him, He just wasn't a priority at the time. I had grown up in church, and figured that I had done my time, so I was old enough to decide that I didn't need to go to church anymore. Instead, I had come to know God on an "in case of emergency" basis. My thought was, that I knew just enough about God that I only needed to contact Him in the event that I was in some kind of trouble. Within three months of being on campus I lost my virginity, started drinking, had no real identity, and God and His church were the furthest things from my mind. I wanted to be loved so desperately that I started looking for love in all of the wrong places. Most of the time when I talked to God, I was either hung-over, praying that I would pass an exam, or scared that I might be pregnant. I relied more on my astrological sign and my peers than I did on God. To say the least, I was lost. After a few years I got tired of crying, tired of hurting, tired of the disappointments, tired of living with no real direction, and thought that just maybe I did need God after all. But what in the world could He do with a mess like me? Could He really clean up the train wreck that I made of myself? Were the plans that He had for me still available for my access? I wasn't sure, but I definitely wanted to find out. The truth was, in spite of my shortcomings, my destiny had already been written, and it was waiting for my arrival.

*   *   *

I love butterflies. Their colors are so beautiful and they fly with such grace. I can't help but smile whenever I see one fly by. When I think about them long enough, I think about the process that they went through to get to that state. The caterpillar had to undergo quite a metamorphosis in order to become a butterfly. If it did not, it would still be inching along the ground, limited in motion and range. Can you imagine if God had given caterpillars free will? I think we would have far less butterflies than we do now. Some would say flying was too risky, some would be comfortable with their low-lying surroundings, some would first want to know every detail of their wings, and some simply may not believe that they would survive such a drastic change.

Unfortunately, so many of us are just like caterpillars with free will. God wants us to get our wings so that the world can marvel at the transformation He's made in us, but we're satisfied inching our way through life. We'll starve our spirits and wonder why we're not growing. We say that Jesus is our Lord and Savior, but yet and still, we look and act exactly the same. We'll marvel at other spiritual leaders, but won't trust God enough to allow Him to take us through a metamorphosis of our own. We're not willing to give up our current bodies and surrender to the transformation that's been predestined for us. So while the butterflies are free to fly as high and as far as they wish, we stay in our caterpillar states, not realizing that we too are destined to fly if we would only allow God to take us through the process.

What is the process? The butterfly cycle consists of four stages: the egg, the larvae, the pupa, and then, the adult. The laying of the egg signifies a new life, which is expected to grow into a butterfly as it reaches adulthood. Before it gets to that point, changes and growth are required during all of the previous stages. During the larva stage, the caterpillar spends most of its time eating and shedding in order to prepare for the drastic change that will take place in the next stage. During the pupa stage, the caterpillar attaches itself to a limb and forms a cocoon in order to prepare for metamorphosis. Once the process is complete, the butterfly emerges, it finds a mate in order to produce more eggs, and the life cycle starts all over.

You may be wondering what the butterfly life cycle has to do with spirituality, and the answer is . . . everything.

When you accept Jesus Christ as your Lord and Savior, the Holy Spirit is placed into your heart. It is a new life that needs to be nourished so that it can grow and replace the old you with the new you. Once God's Spirit hatches inside of you, you need to continue to feed it with His word. As you feed on God's word, your new spirit will continue to grow, and you will shed the things that are not of God. It could be bitterness, resentment, sexual sins, hatred, a host of other things, or maybe a combination of all of the above. How fast you grow will depend on how often you feed on God's word, and your willingness to allow it to work in you. If the only spiritual meal you receive is on Sunday morning, it will take a lot longer for you to mature. If you desire to grow at a faster rate, you will need to feed on the word as often as you can. Your meal could consist of a daily devotion, a designated quiet time with God, a scripture a day, etc. If you desire change and growth, you will need to eat regularly to build up your strength. Once your spirit has matured to the pupa stage, you will find that God wants to become your cocoon. He needs to get you alone and detached from the things that can become distractions such as the media, your friends, and even your own family. It may feel lonely at the time, but you must understand that it's all a part of the process. You are so close to your goal at this point; you can't turn back now. Finally, once God has molded you into exactly what He wants, you will be set free to fly! The world will marvel at the transformation that God has made in you. Your job then is to go out into the world and be a catalyst for the Kingdom, and help to start the life cycle all over again in someone else. That is your ultimate purpose. How you will do it is between you and God.

God's purpose for your life is not about money, fame, or even about you.

How will you know if you're fulfilling God's purpose? God's purpose for your life should be humbling. It is typically something beyond your own abilities, requiring you to depend on Him. God's purpose will glorify Him, not you. If it is something that you can take all of the credit for, then it's possible that you're not fulfilling God's purpose, but rather your own desires. God's purpose may not make you a millionaire, but it will make you rich. God's purpose for your life will meet the needs of others. God's purpose for your life will change you.

Throughout this book, it is my hope that you will not only identify where you are in the spiritual life cycle, but that you will also be led to move forward from wherever you are and discover all that God has called you to be. I am not a pastor, licensed minister or counselor. I am merely an ordinary person who decided to surrender my life to Christ in order to fulfill a purpose greater than myself; a purpose that could have only been revealed by the Spirit of God. I have gone from living life lost and always longing for more, to a life filled with peace and unlimited guidance. After reading this book, I pray that you will allow God to direct your steps so that you too will experience what it's like to live life on purpose. I hope that you will be motivated to deepen your relationship with Him, trust Him, and pursue your calling. I believe that through this book, God wants to set you free. You may be in the egg stage and need help discovering who you are so that you're able to move on to the larva stage. Perhaps you've already accepted Jesus as your Lord and Savior, but your spirit is starving and you're ready for growth. Maybe you've been feeding on the Word, and you know God is calling you for a time of isolation, but you're hesitant due to fear or uncertainty. Or you might already be flying and need to be challenged to initiate new life by saving souls or serving in ministry.

You aren't supposed to spend your life wandering around or feeling empty and unfulfilled. You were created with a purpose in mind; a purpose that has been waiting for your arrival. God wants to transform you, and let the beauty of your soul inspire and motivate those around you to come to know Christ. You have to trust and allow God to take you through the process. You have to be willing to leave the old you behind. God wants to reform you and give you everything you need to come out bigger and better than you were before. No matter where you are in your walk with God, know that you were destined to fly. So get ready, it's time to prepare for flight!

STAGE ONE

The Egg

CHAPTER ONE

New Life

For God so loved the world that he gave his one and only Son, that whoever believes in him shall not perish but have eternal life.

—John 3:16, NIV

New life is so precious and delicate. It is something that must be nurtured and handled with plenty of care. The female butterfly usually lays her eggs on the underside of a leaf in order to provide as much protection as possible[1]. If she were to lay her eggs on the topside of the leaf, any element of nature such as rain or predators could easily harm the new life. My initial thought was, if the butterfly attaches the eggs to the underside of the leaf, wouldn't gravity naturally make it fall? In theory, it would. However, while the eggs are being laid, the butterfly secretes a quick-drying glue-like substance that holds the eggs in place[2]. At that point, the developing larvae can only rely on the yolk and hard outer shell to protect it. Once the egg laying process is complete, the host butterfly will have done all that she could to maximize the chances of the new lives surviving. Air and water are the only external nutrients that the egg receives, which come through a little spore in the egg that was made during fertilization[3].

I remember when I first accepted Jesus into my heart. I was about 13 years old, and I was attending a Christian summer camp called Camp Wabanna, located in Edgewater, MD. Every morning we would start our day out in prayer around the flagpole. We'd have morning devotion, clean our cabins, engage in all sorts of activities during the day like crabbing, swimming, and sailing, and end our days with evening devotion. Our counselor used to play this one tape (as in cassette tape) while we were cleaning up, by a group called Jars of Clay. It was the first time that I had heard Christian Pop/Rock before, so I was already captivated by the unfamiliar sound. There was one song titled "Sinking," that really touched my heart after about the third time I had heard it and really listened to the lyrics.

"Sinking" was a word that described my spiritual life at that time. I was angry, had low self-esteem, was insecure, had feelings of betrayal, and was just overall unhappy on the inside. All of my activities, like dance and bowling, served as escapes from my unhappy reality. I was doing well in school, I had a social life, but I was sinking on the inside. There was a void that needed to be filled, and that void was, a yearning

4

God. So on that third day of camp, after we had finished cleaning, we all gathered for our morning devotion. Typically, before we would close out in prayer, the counselor would ask if anyone wanted to accept Jesus Christ as their Lord and Savior. That day I finally raised my hand. I was Christened as a baby, was required to attend church every Sunday, but I hadn't really formed a relationship with Christ for myself. We said a prayer of salvation and from that moment on the Spirit of God was a part of me. Just like when a mother butterfly lays her egg on a leaf, God had placed the new me inside of my heart.

A seed of new life was planted that would need to be protected and nourished so that it would be able to mature to the next stage. I grew up attending an Episcopalian Church that I considered pretty dry and boring. I think I became an acolyte, or "altar girl" if you will, just to give me something to do during service each week. I was a torch-bearer when I first started out. The biggest thing was, don't catch anything on fire, and don't spill the hot wax. Then as everyone started growing up, the number of acolytes dwindled, so naturally I was promoted to carrying the cross (known as the crucifer). I must admit, I felt pretty important leading the procession down to the altar. The one thing I always wanted to do, but never got the chance, was to be the thurifer. That was the person that carried the incense. I always wanted to see how hard it would be to swing the thurible around and keep all of the coals and incense inside. I'm sure there was some religious meaning behind carrying it, but at the time I just wanted to see if I could do tricks with it! We used to sing songs, go through the same rituals just about every week, and I have no clue what was said during any of the sermons. Nonetheless, the Spirit of God was with me, and I was at least a participant in the worship service each week.

From time to time I would go to my aunt's church, which was an A.M.E. Church (African Methodist Episcopal Church). I loved her church. They had youth Sunday, youth retreats, a different choir for every service each Sunday of the month. The music was a lot more upbeat than in the Episcopal Church, and I could actually understand the sermons. That's where I first saw someone catch the spirit. That was something that would never happen at the Episcopal Church. I mean we were doing well if we clapped during one song! But at my aunt's church, people were falling out of chairs and running around the sanctuary. It got to the point where we could start predicting who was going to start shouting and when. I didn't really understand it, but it was pretty entertaining for a kid to say the least. My activity of choice at her church was singing in the choir. Early on I sang in the children's choir, and then once I became a teenager I sang in the mass choir. They rehearsed on Saturdays, so I was able to fit that in my schedule. At least once a month, I would get to hang up my acolyte robe and go sing with the mass choir. And that's pretty much all I remember about "growing up" in church. If I didn't get anything else, the one thing that I knew was that

I should be in somebody's church every Sunday. However, although I received a basic understanding of "church" while growing up, I didn't have a real understanding of how to build a relationship with Christ. Jesus was in my heart, I knew about going to church and being active in church, I learned about communion, prayer, reading the Bible, and about tithes and offerings. Learning the basics was good, but it wasn't enough to sustain me once I went out into the world on my own. I knew what church was about, but I did not really know what being a Christian was about. Once I graduated from high school, for the next few years, let's just say I decided to take the "scenic" route through life.

Although the Spirit of God was in me, development was slowly taking place. I knew that I needed God in my life, but I didn't know that we were supposed to grow in a relationship with one another. I didn't know that there was a purpose that I was supposed to fulfill. Once I went to college and was free to decide whether or not I was going to church on Sunday, I decided not to go. I figured I had gone to church more than enough over the prior seventeen years of my life, and I had all that I needed to get by in life. Up until that point, I was saved and I was still a virgin, so I was more than prepared for the next stage of my life. Boy, was I wrong. Little did I know, that things were about to go downhill, and quickly.

Although I was involved in activities in high school, I had glasses, braces, and was often made fun of. I was a tomboy, had a flat chest, and was accused of trying to "act white" because

I was in advanced classes and spoke grammatically correct. I still had friends, so I wasn't completely alone, but what kid doesn't want to be liked? The first few boyfriends I did have cheated on me, so my first experience with relationships didn't exactly get off to a great start. Once I started college, it was like a whole new world. A new place, new people, and suddenly, I became blinded by the attention I was getting. The glasses were gone, the braces were off, and I was finally attractive to more than just one person. I wanted to be cool. I wanted to be liked. I wanted to be loved. I figured I could make up for the time I lost while being somewhat of a nerd in high school. Instead, I should have been worried about whether or not my life was attractive to God, rather than trying to attract some guy that just wanted to get me in his bed. Unfortunately, that wasn't the case. I ended up dating this one guy, and was dumb enough to allow him to take me to his room thinking that I would be able to resist temptation. Wrong! One thing led to another, and just like that, I was no longer a virgin. My dream of saving myself for marriage had vanished. The sad thing was, I didn't even enjoy it. I knew that God created sex as something beautiful and sacred for a husband and wife to share. What happened that night made me feel cheap, dirty, and ashamed. The guy didn't even care about the fact that I was a virgin, and instead insisted that I was lying. All of those years I had waited, hoping for something special and instead I encountered one of the worst experiences of my life. After it was all over, all I could do was roll over and cry. I knew that I had disappointed myself and God. The worst part about it was that by the next day, I had gotten over my disappointment. I told God I was sorry, but at that point there was nothing that I could do to get my virginity back. So I thought I might as well keep the party going.

Semester after semester, one one-night stand after another, one bad relationship after another, and many drunken nights sent my spiritual life downhill quickly. It was almost as if I had become addicted to bad behavior. I was numb to disappointing God. I wasn't thinking about Him, and I wasn't trying to. I was losing sight of who I was called to be. The identity that He had given me had become lost in my sins and was covered in disobedience. After all that I had done, I figured it was too late to turn back at that point, so I kept right on living life through my own destructive eyes. That was until I hit rock bottom. I had nearly starved and suffocated the new life that was inside of me. I felt so defeated. I was tired of crying, hurting, not being loved the way that I knew I could be, disobeying God, and just feeling empty. I was causing more trouble for myself than it was worth. I had no idea what my life was about, or the direction I was supposed to be going. I was lost, and I had to finally face the train wreck that I made of myself while trying to go through life on my own. There were no excuses; I had chosen to remove God from my life, and I needed to allow Him back in. At that point, what did I have to lose? I was already broken and unhappy, so things couldn't have gotten any worse than they already were.

I was twenty-four years old when I decided I was finally ready to start developing a relationship with Christ. I didn't exactly know how, but sitting under His word on a weekly basis was a good start. The first Sunday that I went back to church, the very next day, I was told that the pastor quit! I am not kidding. After all that I had been through, I finally took a step in the right direction, and the pastor quits? Wow! I honestly didn't know what to think. I thought, well maybe I was right. God must have really been mad at me, and that was His way of showing it. But I refused to give up. I knew that I needed God, and I was willing to do whatever it was going to take to get back in His presence. I later found out that the pastor that quit actually went on to start a new church. So I really wasn't beyond redemption as I had originally thought. That was a relief! About a month or so later I officially joined the church, and was baptized later that same year right before my twenty-fifth birthday, and made a commitment to get my life back on track. After all of that time I discovered that God never left me. When I sought the love of man more than His love, He was still there. When I nearly cut Him out of my life, He was still there. While I was willfully abusing the temple He gave me, He was still there. Although the space I gave Him to occupy was small, He was still in my heart, and waiting for me to start developing. Just like the glue-like substance that secures the butterfly's egg on a leaf to protect it from washing away in rainy waters, God had kept me, and He wasn't going anywhere. It was time for me to start developing for real. I knew that this time around it had to be more than just about going to church. I needed to know Jesus. I needed Him to be Lord over my life, and to redeem me from the pit I had built for myself.

If you are going to pursue God's purpose for your life, you must acknowledge in your heart that no matter your current circumstances or your past convictions, God set you apart from the very beginning. Before you were conceived, before you were born, before you were given your birth name, God made plans specifically for you[4]. It is God who is still able to give you life even after your failures. When I took a closer look at Adam and Eve in Genesis 3, I saw something different. I noticed that in verse 7, after they had sinned, they sewed together fig leaves to try to cover themselves. But when you get to Genesis 3:21 AMP it says, "For Adam also and for his wife the Lord God made long coats (tunics) of skins and clothed them." God showed me that even after they had sinned, and suffered the consequences, He still covered them better than they could have covered themselves! I believe that he wants to do the same for every one of us. If we would just come out of hiding from beneath all of our sin, guilt, and shame, God will wrap His love around us and cover us even today. In fact, He has made that possible for us through the death of His son, Jesus Christ. His blood covers all of our sins, and is a declaration of God's love for us. You have to be willing to be covered. You can continue to try to live in the shadows of your sin, but you will not experience all that God has for you. You cannot pursue your calling if you are spending most of your time hiding from God. Are you going to keep sewing together fig leaves attempting to patch up your life with your own hands, or will you let God cover you and restore the life that He intended for you to have in the first place?

I hope you know that there is a calling on your life greater than you could even imagine. Every time you see one of your brothers or sisters in Christ fulfilling God's calling, remember that you too were destined to be amongst them, flying high, giving off light to the world. Your destiny may not look exactly like theirs, but God desires to transform you just the same. Just like you, they too have a past. We all do. Whatever it is that you're going through right now, believe in your heart that there's something greater in your future. God wants to take you through a metamorphosis of your own, if you'll surrender to the process. You have a new life inside of you that is waiting to be developed. Think about this, the caterpillar undergoes such a transformation that by the time it's done, he's known by another name altogether. Whatever name your past has given you—adulterer, murderer, fornicator, thief, liar, gossiper, gambler, heathen, drug abuser, pervert, etc.— know that God has a new name waiting for you! Whatever name you've given yourself—failure, unworthy, unqualified, outcast, unattractive, unwanted, loser, victim, etc.—God has a new name waiting for you! You weren't predestined to be any of those things, and it's time to leave them behind so that you can walk in the ways of the Lord. You were predestined to live a life of abundance and righteousness. And when God is done taking you through the process, His Spirit will shine so brightly through you that the old you will be unrecognizable.

Declare this day that by the blood of Jesus Christ you will be called blessed, victorious, renewed, redeemed, pure, anointed, and anything else related to a child of God. Acknowledge today that there is a mission so great with your name on it that even your past can't shut it down. God is calling you forward to a greater life with Him. Your destiny awaits you! The first step in fulfilling God's purpose for your life is to repent of your sins and accept Jesus Christ as your Lord and Savior. Maybe you are like I was; you claimed to be saved, but your actions said otherwise. You can still repent and make Jesus the Lord of your life right now. If you're reading this and you aren't saved, I want to pray with you first. All you have to do is recite the prayer below, and you will receive God's gift of salvation:

Dear God, I acknowledge that I have sinned against you, and I ask for your forgiveness. Today, I turn away from my sins, and turn towards you. I believe that Jesus is Lord and I believe in my heart that you raised Him from the dead. Jesus, I ask that you would come into my heart and save me. Write my name in the lamb's book of life. Lord, I thank you for cleansing me and for giving me new life. Fill me with your Spirit. It's in Jesus' name that I pray, Amen.

If you're reading this, and you're already saved, and want to rededicate your life to Christ, I want to pray with you as well:

Dear God, today I recommit my life to you. I believe that Jesus died for my sins, and I want to make him Lord over my life. I repent of my wicked ways, and ask for your forgiveness. Create in me a clean heart O God, and renew a right spirit within me. I receive your redemption today. It's in Jesus' name that I pray. Amen.

If you prayed either of the above prayers and believed them with your whole heart, congratulations, you received new life today! It's time to leave behind the old, and bring in the new. Get ready to embark on a journey that was designed especially for you. Get ready to grow. Get ready to be transformed. Get ready to give God the glory. We've been waiting!

PREPARING FOR FLIGHT

- Do you believe in your heart that God has redeemed you from your past?
- What sins have been keeping you from growing in your relationship with Christ?
- Are you truly fulfilled and satisfied with the direction in which your life is going?
- Will you lay down your life so that you can pursue God's plans with all of your heart?
- Are you willing to accept God's calling for your life?

Let us pray:

Dear Lord, I thank You for new life and the forgiveness of sins. I thank You for the plans that You have designed especially for me. Lord, today I choose to leave behind my life of sin and surrender to Your will. I trust that Your plans are better than the plans that I have for myself. I ask that You would give me the courage, wisdom, and resources that I need to complete the assignments that lie ahead. May You get all of the glory and honor; it's in Jesus' name that I pray, Amen.

CHAPTER TWO

Church is not Enough

All Scripture is God-breathed and is useful for teaching, rebuking, correcting and training in righteousness, so that the servant of God may be thoroughly equipped for every good work.

—2 Timothy 3:16-17, NIV

It is so important that you protect the new life that God puts inside of you. Remember, you are preparing for flight. Even while writing this, I keep seeing images in my head of an embryo that's being incubated in its mother's womb. A precious life that is so delicate protected mostly by fluid, and with no control over the nutrients that are passed to it. Likewise, the butterfly egg only permits air and water to pass through its shell while developing. Just imagine your heart for a second. Inside of your heart is the spirit of God, in its embryonic state. The spiritual embryo has no control over the nutrients that are being poured into it, only you do. Proverbs 4:23 says, "Above all else, guard your heart, for everything you do flows from it." Whatever is in your heart is passed on to your spirit. The Word of God is filled with everything you need to transform your heart and to help nourish your new life. You are responsible for feeding your spirit, not just your pastor. There are scriptures related to just about every topic you can think of. Most of the topics and some of the rituals that you learn in church can be learned by reading your bible. Going to church just simplifies, condenses it all, and puts it into practice. Whether it's your health, finances, dealing with people, raising a family, prayer, protection, the list goes on and on. God has given us a manual for life, which was designed to guide and protect us. Referring to it once a week leaves a lot of room for error, and may slow down your growth significantly. I'm not saying that going to church is unnecessary; however, I do believe that it is only a small part of your journey. Let's take a closer look as to why you'll need to pursue God as much outside of church as inside of church.

It's Not About Religion. It's About Relationship.

Your new life is about more than just going to church. In fact, it's about more than your salvation and hoping to go to Heaven when you die. Those things are great, but they are just a smaller part of a bigger picture. I believe that your growth and purpose will be limited if going to church is the extent of your relationship with God. I didn't know that I was supposed to evolve into a new creature altogether. I thought the whole point of salvation was to save your own soul from eternal damnation by believing in Jesus, and that was it. Because I didn't develop beyond salvation or have a real relationship with God, as soon as I left church I found myself worse off than I was before I got saved. Not only had I let my guard down, but it became almost nonexistent. Learning about religion and practicing rituals didn't prepare me for the road that was ahead of me. I was not in church when God revealed His purpose for my life. He revealed it to me while I was at home having my own bible study and prayer time. God's purpose for your life may not have anything to do with the church in and of itself. You may serve in ministry at church, but God's purpose is for you to be a light unto the world, not just to other Christians. You could be the light that changes the face of how corporations conduct business. Your purpose might be to travel the world as a missionary. You could be used to discover a medical breakthrough. You may birth a ministry out of your love for fashion, food, finances, the arts, etc. The possibilities are endless! The good news is God will lead you exactly where He needs you to be!

I didn't have a choice but to go to church when I was growing up. I wasn't going because I was so in love with God and had some deep desire to serve Him. I was going because I had to, and historically, our family was expected to go to church. Unfortunately, going to church doesn't change people, a relationship with God does. Although I am thankful for having learned about the Christian religion, the one thing that I was missing, but needed the most, was a relationship with Christ. He was supposed to become the head of my life. In some ways, church can be seen as simply an avenue by which people come together to share their beliefs, fellowship, and worship. Atheists can have church if they want to. There is even a "church" of scientology. My point is, going to church does not make you a follower of Christ. If you are going to pursue your purpose, you need to make sure that you are seeking a relationship with Christ in conjunction with your religious practices.

Giving was one of the first things I did to begin developing a deeper relationship with Christ. I knew that if I could trust God with my money, our relationship could only go up hill from there. I know that there are some churches that seem to beg for its members to give money. However, people should give because of their relationship with God; it's not something that they can be pressured into by the pastor. 2 Corinthians 9:7 says, "Each of you should give what you have decided in your heart to give, not reluctantly or under compulsion, for God loves a cheerful giver." If you do belong to a church, you should be giving tithes and offerings. Until you decide in your heart to trust and worship God with your finances, you simply won't give with a pure heart, or you might not give at all. If you aren't giving, I believe it is a sign that you are disconnected from God. As you continue to grow your relationship with Christ and gain greater understanding, giving will become a by-product of your spiritual growth. You will be more willing to give your time, talent, and treasure as God changes your heart and you desire to become a better servant for the Kingdom. Remember, the foundation of your purpose is built upon your relationship with God.

Take a look at the function that church serves in our life. Is it something on your to-do list? Is it simply a matter of tradition? Is it an outward expression of your desire to worship and serve God? While there are many types of churches, I recommend that you worship with other people that are under the submission of Christ and can meet you on your level. Don't just go once a week because it's some habit that you were taught to form. You should expect to hear from God and draw closer to Him while you're there. Get involved, and build up your faith. Make sure that you are developing a relationship and not just practicing religion. The point is, don't get so caught up in church traditions that you miss out on a greater calling. Spend time with Him daily and seek to deepen your relationship with Him both inside and outside of church.

Everyone Is Different

Isn't it interesting that some people have been going to church all of their lives but they haven't changed? They're still mean, they're still not giving, they're still not serving, they're still not pursuing the things of God, they're still disobedient, etc. How can that be? It's because they haven't unleashed the power that's inside of them. Just because you get saved, that doesn't automatically mean that you'll change. You have a choice to pursue God or to keep living life as you were. When we look at Ephesians 3:20, it says, "Now to him who is able to do immeasurably more than all we ask or imagine, according to his power that is at work within us." God has to be working in you in order for you to fulfill his purpose for your life. If not, his Spirit is just sitting dormant inside of your heart.

Everyone in church is in different stages of the spiritual life cycle. Some are just starting out and some are in later stages of development. As you try to discover God's purpose for your life, do not be fooled, everyone in church is not operating where they should be. What you may witness for one or two hours is not enough to determine the totality of a person's spiritual life. That doesn't mean that you set out to try and uncover who's real and who's merely acting. The point is, don't let your perceptions of other people hinder your walk with God. God has placed something special inside of you, and you are no less deserving than the next person to have such a great gift. You do not have to be perfect to be involved in church; it's impossible for you to be. However, if you truly have a heart for God and want to allow Him to work in your life, then go for it. The more light you add, the brighter we all will become.

Your light may be dim right now, but God wants to make it brighter. We all have our struggles, and God can work equally in all of us. Through God's grace, He allows us all to come together for a greater good—His Kingdom. Yes, even you.

When I decided to go back to church I was trying to find my way back to God. I eventually found Him, but I was still going to the club, still dabbling in astrology, still trying to find myself, still cussing, and still doing a lot of the same things I was doing before. Why? It's because I wasn't developing on the inside. The little egg that had been planted in my heart was still just an egg. What I needed had very little to do with practicing religion, and everything to do with getting to know God for myself. Once my relationship with God started to develop, that's when I started to change. You may not ever go to church, and still have some type of a relationship with God. You can still pray, study scripture, worship, etc. Inversely, you can go to church your entire life and still not know God. You might know of Him, but your heart will have remained the same. When I went through my stint of being anti-church it was because of bad experiences with the people on the inside. I let their behaviors drive me away. I just expected so-called Christians to treat me better than non-Christians that I had encountered. I expected them to exemplify Christ, and that wasn't the case. In looking back, I wasn't displaying Godly behavior either. I was being judgmental, instead of being patient and extending the same grace and love that God had given me. But as an immature Christian, I wasn't able to understand that at the time. God didn't give me that revelation until many years later. I repented, and I now try to be more patient with those that have not yet reached their full potential. I have a better understanding of why people are the way that they are; however, being judgmental was counter-productive to my own growth.

Should Christians live by higher standards? Yes, they should. Just don't let the ones that choose otherwise affect your decision to pursue God for yourself.

You Need A Well-Balanced Spiritual Diet

Sermons can just be snapshots and individual interpretations of the bible based on the background of the preacher. Whatever you hear in church, you should also study for yourself. You should be so filled with the word during the week that sermons become confirmations and supplements of your own study. Gaining knowledge from one type of gospel won't be enough. You need a well-balanced spiritual diet. You need to receive word on obeying God's commands as well as on His benefits and blessings. You need to receive word on how to treat others. Just as your natural diet does not only consist of sweets and candy, neither should your spiritual diet. Your vegetables may not taste good, but it doesn't mean they aren't good for you. Likewise, we may not like God's word to convict us, but it doesn't mean that we don't need it for spiritual growth. Make sure that you are receiving well-balanced teachings from whatever sources you choose. If your pastor only preaches on prosperity, find teachings on righteousness. If your church only produces fire and brimstone messages, then study teachings on redemption and restoration. Learn about the benefits of prayer and fasting, healing, and every other area that you can. You and God will both play a role in this journey. Therefore, knowledge of both roles will be essential in preparing to fly in your purpose.

Although going to church isn't everything, I do believe that you should have a church home. There are many benefits to belonging to a church such as worshipping with other Christians, serving in ministry, networking, creating a support system, witnessing to unbelievers, and gaining deeper knowledge and understanding. I recommend that you become a part of a church that teaches biblical truths and professes that Jesus is their Lord and Savior if you have not already done so.

Some of you may have heard horror stories or maybe you've been hurt in church before, but let God speak to your heart. This is coming from someone that once despised the church and everything that it stood for. I compared the life of people that didn't go to church to people that did go, and somehow concluded that life outside of church was better. I mean at least they were honest about it. Quite frankly, I was treated better by people that didn't go to church than by ones that did! Why would I want to associate myself with a bunch of hypocrites when I could just live my life outside of the church and still deal with everyday issues? It just didn't make any sense to me. I was willing to let the behaviors of others come in between my relationship with God. And I found out, it was not worth it. We are all a work in progress, and God will meet you right where you are. I'm telling you, negative thoughts will mess with your head and your heart if your relationship with God isn't secure. They will attempt to drive you away from the one thing that you need most, and that is God. That moment you think you don't need to maintain your relationship with Christ you actually lay out a welcoming mat for the devil to enter into your spirit.

Once you join a church, connect with a group of Christians that share in your interest of pursuing Christ wholeheartedly. Some people get saved and then sit back and hide, or keep to themselves wondering what's next. Sometimes the guilt of our past or present situations can keep us isolated or secluded. Whether you're single or married, find out if there are other singles or married couples your age. Maybe there's a group of people with similar hobbies or sports interests. Just know that you don't have to go through this alone. You have a lot of growing to do, and there will be people that will support you along the way. You should keep as much positive energy flowing as possible, and surround yourself with people that will speak life into you and your walk with Christ.

If you've stopped going to church, let God guide you back to where you were going or ask him to lead you somewhere new. If you've never gone to church, now is a good time to start.

Pray to God about how you feel. He knows what you've been through and will go to great lengths to have you back by His side. Pray that He would dissolve any stigmas that you have against the church. Pray that He would heal your wounds from anyone that's hurt you. It may take you some time to find a church that you like, or to recover from past hurts, and that's ok. But I believe that you should have a church home, where you can serve and sit under sound biblical teachings on a regular basis. You may even be able to subscribe to a church online or listen to podcasts to get you started. At the very least, this will help you get the nutrients flowing to the new life that's inside of you. After I was saved, I may not have understood Scripture in its entirety, or known any prayers besides the Lord's Prayer, but sitting under regular teaching helped jumpstart the development process.

It's not about what church has the best choir, the most members, or the most popular pastor. It's about what church is equipping its people to do the work of the Kingdom as discussed in the following verses:

- Ephesians 4:11-13, "So Christ himself gave the apostles, the prophets, the evangelists, the pastors and teachers, to equip his people for works of service, so that the body of Christ may be built up until we all reach unity in the faith and in the knowledge of the Son of God and become mature, attaining to the whole measure of the fullness of Christ."

- 2 Timothy 3:16-17, "All Scripture is God-breathed and is useful for teaching, rebuking, correcting and training in righteousness, so that the servant of God may be thoroughly equipped for every good work.
- Hebrews 13:20-21, "Now may the God of peace, who through the blood of the eternal covenant brought back from the dead our Lord Jesus, that great Shepherd of the sheep, equip you with everything good for doing his will, and may he work in us what is pleasing to him, through Jesus Christ, to whom be glory for ever and ever. Amen.

I did not know what my prayer life should look like, how to study the bible, or how to identify my spiritual gifts, much less know if they even existed in this day and age. Needless to say, I was not fully equipped for my journey. That is not to say that learning ever stops; however, there are basics that should be learned and studied at the onset of becoming a Christian or rededication of your life to Christ. The church is responsible for filling in that gap for the married, singles, teens, elderly, and children alike serving as a resource center for believers. We are to challenge each other to live righteously and also provide tools for doing so. Church isn't just about Sunday morning worship; it should be a learning and development center for discipleship.

Make sure that your church provides a learning environment with sound guidelines for Christian living. Ask about a curriculum. Are you able to take what you learn at church and apply it to your home or work environment? Are you growing in the things of God? Are you confident and comfortable enough to share your faith with others?

Will you ever find a "perfect" church? No, because all of them are filled with humans. Even so, your journey is between you and God. Above all else, you have to protect the new life inside of you with God's Word, worship, and prayer. Attending church is a part of that process and can be a great resource for you. However, if you're going to pursue God's purpose for your life you will need more than church.

Going to church should be a by-product of your relationship with Christ, not the extent of it. If you are skeptical about the people in church, turn your judgments into prayers, so that you can keep your heart pure before God. As you pray for yourself, pray for others. Set the example wherever you are. Be what God has called you to be, which is light in the midst of darkness. Instead of comparing yourself to other Christians, your litmus test should be the Word and Spirit of God. Does your life reflect the world's views or God's? Are you following God's will or your own desires? Are you serving in a particular ministry because it's popular, you like the people in the group, it's something that you "like," or because your spiritual gifts and God led you there? I'll review spiritual gifts later on in chapter 4.

I just want to be clear that fulfilling God's purpose for your life is not about pursuing church; it's about pursuing God.

You have to protect the gift that's inside of you by learning all areas of the bible, not just a few. You have to desire to be transformed. You have to start with the end in mind. The end is not church. The end is becoming all that God has called you to be. Will you be thoroughly equipped for the journey?

PREPARING FOR FLIGHT

- Are you a member of a church? Why or why not?
- If you are a member of a church, what types of teachings are you sitting under?
- How balanced is your spiritual diet? In what areas do you need to expand your study?
- Will you keep your salvation to yourself or will you be the light that will draw others to Christ?
- What will you have to show for living a life with Christ? Church attendance or completed assignments?

Let us pray:

Lord, I understand that my salvation is about more than just going to church. I pray that you would search my heart and release it of any judgment that I have on church and its members. I believe that you are able to work in all of us, and I ask you to do so. If there is any area of my worship that I could improve, please reveal it to me. Whether it is in my giving, serving others, prayer, or studying your Word, I seek only to please you. It's in Jesus' name that I pray, Amen.

CHAPTER THREE

Destined to Fly

For we are God's handiwork, created in Christ Jesus
to do good works, which God prepared in advance
for us to do.

—Ephesians 2:10, NIV

When we look at the butterfly, we know that it wasn't born that way. The butterfly is the result of a caterpillar undergoing a complete transformation through a process called metamorphosis. What once was a furry, worm-like creature, limited to inching along the ground, risking being stepped on by humans, and falling prey to predators like birds, turned into the beautiful insect able to fly higher and farther than its initial surroundings. Whether the caterpillar knows it or not, the body that he's in is predestined for transformation. If he merely focuses on his current state, what features he doesn't have, or his limited abilities, he'll slow down his own growth. His path has already been prepared for him; he just needs to make it through all of the stages of the process, and he too will fly amongst the other butterflies. If he only pays attention to the fact that in his current state he lacks the ability to fly or that his current body looks nothing like that of the butterfly's, he won't be able to take full advantage of the state that he's in, which is preparing him for flight. He has to start with the end in mind, and keep his eye on the prize.

The Spirit of God is the seed from which everything else within you will develop. Your spiritual gift or gifts have already been determined, your path has been drawn, and your destiny has been prepared. Just like the little caterpillar that's inside of the butterfly egg the type of butterfly it will become has already been determined by the host that laid the egg. The caterpillar will not be able to determine its size, the color, or the detail of its wings. When you accept God's Spirit into your heart, everything else that unfolds has already been determined by the host, God. 2 Corinthians 3:18 says, "And we all, who with unveiled faces contemplate the Lord's glory, are being transformed into his image with ever-increasing glory, which comes from the Lord, who is the Spirit." Before you accepted him, He already knew your talents, how they would be used to glorify him, and the path to your destiny. That never changes. How and when we get there is determined by our rate of spiritual growth, faith, trust, obedience, and relationship with God. While we may never fully activate the Spirit of God in our lives, it doesn't negate the fact that there is a predestined path for us to follow.

Imagine you've been given the task of outlining a path from point A (where you are right now), to point B (a location you've never seen or visited). You cannot use directions; you can only depend on yourself. If you can figure out in which direction you need to go, you may have some idea of the quickest way to get there or you may have no clue at all. If you have somewhat of an idea, you may be able to follow your instincts as far as they'll take you before having to pull over and rely on outside resources to get you through the remainder of the trip. If you have absolutely no clue where you're going, good luck. If you start driving you'll end up somewhere eventually. It may not be exactly where you should have ended up, but you will have arrived at some destination. Now, think about how much easier it is to take a road trip to a place you've never been when you have directions or a GPS guiding you. In the beginning all you may know are your start and end points. Once you click the button that says "get directions," the gap between the two points has been filled with interstate names, specific exits, street names, etc., all the way to your destination. What seemed nearly impossible before, has now become more clear and attainable. That's exactly what the journey to God's destiny for your life is like. God has already determined "point B" in your life, and the Spirit of God will be your GPS. You can either go through life based on your own instincts and end up somewhere, you can follow the path of the crowd, or you can rely on God's GPS to get you to exactly where he wants and needs you to be.

One thing I don't like is driving around lost. I hate to waste gas while racking up additional miles making U-turns, getting back on and off highways, etc. Not to mention the frustration that I feel. I just want to get where I'm going and call it a day. What's worse is when I'm so close to my destination, and one wrong turn puts me at least another twenty to thirty minutes out of my way.

Just recently I went to visit a friend that lives in Washington, D.C. Mind you, I've been to her house several times, and could easily find my way. For some reason I doubted myself and decided to get directions from the maps app on my phone. I made it to D.C., was about 10 minutes away from her house, and decided to refer back to the directions my phone had given me. There's always so much construction going on in that area that I wanted to make sure that the route hadn't changed. When I read them, I knew that they weren't quite the same directions that I had remembered, but since I used the app many times before, I figured the phone was right. Wrong! Once I got turned around, I figured I knew the area well enough that I could "feel" my way to her house. Wrong again! I ended up driving around for an extra ten to fifteen minutes, livid, before I finally ended up calling my friend and had her guide me to her house. She literally had to get in her car, come find me, and then lead me to her house! We laughed about it later, but I didn't find anything humorous about the situation while it was happening.

Life can be the same way. We know the directions that God has given us, but when doubt and fear enter our hearts and minds, we can sometimes turn to external resources that may not reflect what God has already revealed to us. Had I trusted my instincts, I would have made it to her house on time, but doubt and fear ended up leaving me confused and lost. A place that was usually familiar, all of a sudden "appeared" to be unfamiliar territory. In reality, it was a route that I knew like the back of my hand, but in my mind, fear had created a totally different image.

In order to follow God, you will have to trust him wholeheartedly. The opinions of others, doubt, and fear, can knock you off course in the blink of an eye if you allow it. However, if you do happen to go off course, cry out to Him, and he will send you help to get you back on track. In Matthew 14:29-30, when Peter started to sink after attempting to walk on water, he cried out, "Lord, save me!" He didn't just keep sinking hoping that he would eventually save himself or turn to the men that were still in the boat. He called out to the One that could actually do something about his situation! Your friends can't save you, your spouse can't save you, and you can't even save yourself. So no matter what happens along your journey, keep the end in sight, and always refer back to God when in doubt.

And let's be clear, maturing to spiritual adulthood isn't the end all, be all to your journey with Christ. There will still be more work, more growing, more trials, and even more work required of you. Consider the words of the Apostle Paul in Philippians 3:12-14 (NIV):

> "Not that I have already obtained all this, or have already arrived at my goal, but I press on to take hold of that for which Christ Jesus took hold of me. Brothers and sisters, I do not consider myself yet to have taken hold of it. But one thing I do: Forgetting what is behind and straining toward what is ahead, I press on toward the goal to win the prize for which God has called me heavenward in Christ Jesus."

Maturing in Christ is just half the battle. It simply symbolizes the fact that you've made the commitment to press forward in the things of God. Instead of trying to go through life blind, based on your own feelings and instincts, you've surrendered to the Spirit and will of God. Instead of following in the footsteps of your friends and family, you're laying the footsteps of God's path for your life. You're less likely to be swayed by what is popular and what is currently trending in society because you're focused on your destiny. Spiritual growth is ongoing; and anyone who thinks that they have "arrived" at any point is highly mistaken and misguided.

While you're following God and allowing him to transform you along the way, it may seem like you're all alone at times, it might feel as if you're going in the wrong direction, or that you're not moving fast enough. There will be people that won't fully understand your calling, but God knows what He's doing. He's the one that knew you before you were born. He's the one that made you. There will be checkpoints along the way to reassure you that you should keep going. If you are unsure, refer back to your spiritual GPS, the Holy Spirit.

I'll admit that the "look" of a mature Christian can be intimidating in the beginning. It was for me. How can someone that just accepted Jesus Christ participate in ministry? Was I worthy enough to hear from God? Would God actually listen to and answer my prayers? The other people had been doing the church thing for years, and there was no way that I was "qualified" to be amongst them. It was nothing but a lie from the devil. You simply have to ignore him. He doesn't qualify you; God does.

You have to remember, now that you're saved, the devil is going to try to attack you. He doesn't have to worry about those that aren't pursuing God because they're already doing his dirty work for him. The devil didn't need to try and destroy me when I was living in sin because I had already put myself on a path of destruction. But once I became serious about God, I also became a threat to the prince of darkness. I felt like every time I wanted to do the right thing, I was always tempted with the wrong thing. Guys that I was trying get over would pop up out of the blue and so forth. You will have to fight through temptations, so make sure that you protect your heart and mind through prayer, and stay on guard at all times.

There are quite a few "before & after" testimonies that I have read regarding God's transformation process. I used to be so intimidated and disappointed that I wasn't as spiritually mature as the people in the stories were. Ok, I wasn't anywhere close to being where they were. It just seemed like they were so holy and could do no wrong. Often times, I would feel jealous and unworthy. I would read different Christian blogs looking for some sense of direction and inspiration. They were inspiring for a while, until I started comparing my own life to theirs. Once I did that, I was no longer being inspired, but I was being deflated. I just wasn't sure that God would turn this big mess named "me" into a message like He had done for them. It's so easy to get caught up in someone else's life and miss out on your own if you're not careful. But God made me realize that those people were the butterflies that He placed in my life. I had heard a pastor say that I was comparing someone else's highlight reel to my behind the scenes. And he was right. It wasn't that I was any less qualified than they were, but I was merely comparing apples to oranges, as the saying goes. God hadn't led me to those people to make me feel bad about myself; He led me to them so that He could give me hope, inspiration, and motivation. He led me to them to show me living proof of His power at work. We can all live holy lives if we are willing to live by His Spirit. God also told me that I was right, I wasn't worthy. None of us are, but that's not what He was looking for. He just wanted me to be willing: willing to trust Him, willing to surrender to His will, and willing to leave my life of sin and pursue the calling that He placed on my life. I was ready, but in order to pursue my calling, I first had to find out what my calling was.

After I committed to seek God with my whole heart, I purchased a Bible, New International Version, which I could both understand and was still close to the original writings. I also bought a journal to write down my thoughts. In order to get to know God and His plans, I was going to have to start spending time with Him, read and study His Word, and communicate with Him regularly through prayer. I was uncomfortable with my quiet time at first because it was something that I had never done before. I wasn't sure what scriptures to study, how I should talk to God, or if He could even hear me. Sometimes I would go to the index and look up scriptures on a specific topic, other times I would just randomly turn to a page and just start reading. My method didn't really matter; God just wanted my heart, and I was willing to give it to him.

A few days into my studies, I just sat in my room and asked God to tell me what He had planned for my life. I saw myself speaking in front of a large group of people, and I was helping them find their purpose in life. Now keep in mind, I'm an introvert. At the time, I was absolutely terrified of public speaking and could barely understand my own spiritual gifts, let alone help someone else with theirs. Was I hearing from God or was it just my imagination? I wasn't sure, but I just knew that I hadn't heard correctly. I thought my calling was supposed to be something that I liked doing, and speaking in front of people definitely wasn't one of those things. Nonetheless, I wrote down what I thought God had said, closed my journal, and went back to my life as it was. That incident occurred back in February of 2008. I didn't actually pursue the vision until 3 years later.

You can run from God's calling on your life, but you can't hide from it. It will continue to find its way back to you because it lives inside of you. It may continue to reveal itself through an ongoing feeling of emptiness or by small gentle whispers and nudges. No matter how much I hated the thought of having to speak publicly, it was what God had called me to do. I could either keep running or I could finally surrender to God's will.

I chose to stop running and finally surrendered. Not only was I terrified but I was curious to see how He was going to work this thing out. I told God that I would do what He wanted, as long as He prepared me for it. Did I run out and quit my job? No. That wasn't a part of the current plan. Sometimes we can be so quick to change course that we still miss out on what God has for us. Instead, I was patient because God needed me to grow and develop right where I was. Before you start looking for a way out of your current job, educational pursuit, etc., ask God if there is a work for you to do right where you are. Let Him lead you. You don't have to force God's plans to happen; you just need to walk in them.

The first thing I needed to do was to get over my fear of public speaking. I joined a public speaking organization called Toastmasters, and survived the first manual that contained ten speeches. The setting was quite intimate, there were about 10-15 members in our group, and most of the speeches were supposed to be between three to five minutes. The first couple of speeches started off a little shaky, but then about half way through, I had found my voice. All of a sudden I didn't need notes, I didn't need to clench to the podium, and I was getting more and more comfortable. I thought, OK God, maybe I can do this after all. I still wasn't all that thrilled about it, but I wanted to be obedient.

Since I was doing so well within my group, I wanted to practice using my skills outside of the club as well. I decided to volunteer as a leader at my church for a program designed to get families and individuals out of debt. I didn't have to talk much, but leading discussions for people that I may or may not have known was still a little nerve-racking to me. However, my heart for helping people change their lives was greater than my own fear. The first step that I took, led right to another. During the time that I was leading the class, and working towards paying off my last student loan, the Lord told me to start a blog. I was really hesitant about doing so because I'm a pretty private person, but again, I wanted to obey God. I titled the blog Riches and Glory, and I started giving biblically based financial advice. It was cool in the beginning, as I was just enjoying the fact that I was operating in God's will. After a while, I started comparing my blog views to some others, and my heart sank. Here I was pouring my heart out, and I barely had 100 views per week, if that many. So, I thought, maybe I hadn't heard God correctly. It seemed as if nobody cared about my topic, and maybe I was just wasting my time.

I let God know how I was feeling, and to give me some kind of sign that I was moving in the right direction. Within a few days, a woman down in the Virgin Islands had thanked me for blessing and inspiring her with my blog. That one person was the light of hope that I needed to keep me going. Even if she was the only person reading, my efforts were worthwhile.

Your calling may not bless the entire world in the beginning. What I learned was that God was testing my heart. Was I really in it for Him, or was I in it for my own selfish reasons? Would I continue to obey him even if I thought that nobody was looking? Through my blog, I learned that my calling wasn't about fame or competition, but it was about my heart and my relationship with God. If you're seeking God's purpose for your life because you want to become famous and have nice things, you're doing it for the wrong reasons.

I'm not saying that those things can't be by-products of your obedience, because they can be. However, they may not be. Your specific calling may not make you an international superstar, but it could make you a hometown hero. You have to be ok with that. The goal here is to fulfill God's purpose for your life, not the purpose you created for yourself based on what others think or how they have been rewarded. God's purpose for your life isn't supposed to look like someone else's. God designed your purpose especially for you!

In 2012, I was invited to speak at my first women's conference. I thought to myself, whoa, I'm not ready for that yet. I had only been speaking in front of groups with 20 people or less. I wasn't ready to address an entire room full of women. I definitely didn't think that I was qualified either. After all, I didn't hold any significant titles, I was still in the early stages of spiritual growth, and I was intimidated by that. I went to God in prayer, He told me not to worry, and that He would be there with me. I realized that He hadn't called me based on a title or lack thereof. He called me because of my heart to serve.

When you truly seek God with all of your heart, He will start to open up doors that will allow you to start walking in your purpose. I didn't think I was ready or holy enough at that point, but to God, I was in the perfect condition to be used by Him. Your confidence and your faith will be tested, but know that you can go to God when you need Him to calm your fears. No matter how big or small the task, remind yourself that you are never alone, and that God is with you. He doesn't need you to be perfect; He just wants you to be intentional about serving Him. If you start planting the seeds, God will make them grow.

After much prayer and preparation, I made it through the conference. There were about 100 women there, and it actually went well. For the first time I really understood the meaning of Philippians 4:7, "And the peace of God, which transcends all understanding, will guard your hearts and your minds in Christ Jesus." I wasn't completely comfortable with my calling, but I was at peace knowing that God was with me, and He was in control. In part, my vision had come true. It wasn't the exact replica yet, but I knew that I was on the right path.

While I was drowning in my world of sin, I never would have thought that I would be sharing a stage with a national gospel recording artist, pastors, and other women who were well-known for changing lives. Could I have seen myself with a heart for changing lives? Not in a million years. Without a relationship with Christ I honestly don't know what my life would look like right now. I don't mean just being "saved," I mean actively pursuing God. I was so-called "saved" while I was doing everything but honoring God. Where I am right now is due to nothing short of the grace of God; yet I still have so much more growing to do! Did I have to put myself through the pain that I suffered just to get here? No. I could have tapped into my calling years ago, but my sin got in the way. You simply cannot pursue God's calling for your life and remain the same. God is in the transformation business. Although we are all born sinners, He has given us access to a pure life through Jesus Christ. At some point, you have to choose whether or not you are going to follow Him wholeheartedly or stay as you are.

The butterfly lays its eggs with the expectation of producing more butterflies, not just caterpillars. As such, we should have the same expectation of ourselves. Our salvation was meant for redemption, restoration, and transformation, not so that we could abuse God. We think we can just keep living our lives any kind of way, continue to ask for unlimited forgiveness, grace, and mercy, and that's good enough. With that mindset, you will not fulfill God's purpose for your life. Your true destiny will lie untouched, and you will remain in a caterpillar-like state, living beneath your God-given potential. You were predestined to be used by God. You may not understand it, you may not like it at first, but trust Him. Where God wants to take you is higher and farther than you could ever take yourself. The question is will you let Him?

If you're new to spending quiet time with God, a good way to start is to search for scriptures in areas such as prayer, forgiveness, obedience, seeking God and His wisdom, and learning how to hear His voice. One particular scripture that I love is Jeremiah 29:13. It says, "You will seek me and find me when you seek me with all your heart." I believe that God's Word is true, so I knew that if I searched for Him through His Word long enough, I would eventually start to hear from Him.

Another scripture to keep in mind as you seek God is James 1:5-8 that says:

> "If any of you lacks wisdom, you should ask God, who gives generously to all without finding fault, and it will be given to you. But when you ask, you must believe and not doubt, because the one who doubts is like a wave of the sea, blown and tossed by the wind. That person should not expect to receive anything from the Lord. Such a person is double-minded and unstable in all they do."

When you go to God, you have to be "all in" as some would say. You have the ability to hear from God through the Holy Spirit. You have to believe it in order to receive it. The voice that you hear will either be God or it won't be. It may be your own voice or maybe even the devil trying to implant negative thoughts. More times than not, when I think I'm not hearing from God, I'm right, and when I think I am hearing from God, I'm right. But I had to learn not to doubt. It didn't happen right away. Sometimes I would think that I was hearing from God, I'd follow through with an act, only to find out that it wasn't Him. How disappointing that would be! I would have a gut feeling that it wasn't Him, but I wasn't one hundred percent sure. Like the scripture said, I did feel unstable during those times because I didn't know which voice to listen to. I would go back and forth in my mind, and by the time I was done I would be so mentally exhausted that I would just take a risk and hope for the best. But I didn't give up, and neither should you. The next time I was unsure, instead of acting right away, I waited. Over time, I learned how to be still before making hasty decisions. Even then, sometimes I would still have to go with my gut and wait for the outcome.

Exercising your faith will feel like you're taking a risk at times, and that's because you are. However, your faith will only get stronger the more you exercise it. Remember, you're going through a process, you're learning, and you're growing. The plans for your life already exist; you just have to learn how to tap into the resource you need to guide you through them. Be patient, be persistent, and no matter what, keep seeking God!

PREPARING FOR FLIGHT

- Think about how much easier it is to drive while using directions. What are some ways your spiritual GPS can help you right now?
- What do you sense that God is calling you to do? How does He want to use you to change lives?
- Will you schedule your daily quiet time with God starting today?
- Are you able to hear God's voice? If so, how can you tell? If not, continue to study God's word and ask God to reveal Himself to you.

Let us pray:

Lord, I want to learn how to hear your voice. I ask that you declutter my heart and my mind so that I may draw closer to you. Show me how to be still so that you can reveal to me the plans that you have for my life. Lord, I trust your Holy Spirit, and surrender to your guidance. I want to make myself available to be used by you. I know that you have the ability to take me higher than I could ever take myself. Today I believe and receive that you predestined me for flight, so that I may bring glory to your name. It's in Jesus' name that I pray, Amen.

CHAPTER FOUR

Get Ready to Hatch

Before I formed you in the womb I knew [and] approved of you [as My chosen instrument], and before you were born I separated and set you apart, consecrating you; [and] I appointed you as a prophet to the nations.

—Jeremiah 1:5, Amplified Version

Great! You're saved, you know you're predestined for greatness, and God supposedly has these wonderful plans for your life. Now, what exactly does all of this have to do with you? Knowing who you are in Christ is just the beginning of the journey. The remainder of your journey will involve you actually pursuing the calling that's on your life.

When a butterfly egg is about to hatch, it takes on a visible change. The egg starts to change color, and the caterpillar's head begins poking at the top in order to get out[1]. Likewise, you should start to see some visible changes in your life. You should be praying and studying God's word more. Some activities in which you participate, shows you watch, and places you go should look less appealing than they did before. If you were feeling lost before, you should have some sense of direction. Whatever it is, something inside of you should be starting to change.

Until I became serious about pursuing God's will for my life, I was led by the desires of my flesh, my Myers-Briggs test scores, my astrological sign, opinions of others, the media, etc. I had never even thought about asking God what He wanted me to do. Back then, I didn't know that He had specific plans for my life that I was supposed to follow. When I was younger, I would always say that I wanted to be an obstetrician when I grew up. I had that dream in mind all the way through high school. I even applied to colleges that had pre-med programs. I can't exactly remember why I picked that profession. I think back then I thought it was pretty cool to be responsible for helping people deliver babies. Other than that, I have no clue where I got the idea.

My freshman year of college at Elon University, I barely passed my first two entry-level chemistry classes with D's. I would always get A's in the labs, but I had a hard time with the actual tests and coursework. I figured if I could barely pass the basic courses, there was no way that I was going to excel in the advanced ones. So I made the decision to meet with my counselor to discuss switching majors. We looked at my Myers-Briggs test results, which were INTJ, and looked at the professions that were associated with it. I liked psychology, so I went with that. The psychology route definitely turned out far better than pre-med, and thankfully I was still able to graduate with a B average. Even though I was proud of my accomplishment, then became the question, "What next?"

In order to make any decent money in my field, I was going to have to get a master's degree at a minimum, and then a doctorate. There were so many different disciplines that I couldn't decide which one I wanted to pursue. I looked at marriage and family therapy, sports psychology, and maybe a few others. Since I couldn't make up my mind, I went on the job search. The summer after I graduated, I ended up working as a sales assistant for a radio broadcasting company for a couple of years. I knew that I wouldn't be there long, as the position had nothing to do with my major, and I wasn't really interested in working in radio.

About three years later, naturally, I started thinking, what next? At the time, I had just started to reconnect with God, but I was still out in the world, lost, in a bad relationship, and just trying to feel my way through life. I left the radio station and went to work for a private marketing company while pursuing an MBA in human resource management part-time. Was I supposed to be pursuing a degree in HR? I honestly didn't know, but I felt like I was making progress according to society's standards. I was told that if I planned on climbing the corporate ladder then I was going to need a master's degree. So I picked a field and ran with it. I wasn't sure where I was headed career-wise; I was just happy that I wasn't where I used to be.

A new beginning also led to another new soul search. I started pulling all of my resources together to try and figure out who I was and to discover my real purpose. I studied all of the attributes of a Scorpio, delved deeper into my Myers-Briggs results, and tried to make some sense of the results of my spiritual gifts assessment. Who was I? What was I supposed to be doing? Was I headed in the right direction? Did I really have a purpose?

Once I got to college, I really started to identify with my astrological sign; so much so, that I decided to get a tattoo of a Scorpio symbol. After all, the attributes that I read described me perfectly, so it was very easy for me to relate to that identity. Scorpios are known to be secretive, hold grudges, are supposedly the "sex sign," loyal, vindictive, possessive, and the list goes on. I could see myself in my sign. The only issue was, that wasn't who God called me to be. Not all of their traits are negative, but those were the ones that I identified with the most at that time. God tells us to forgive, not to hold grudges. I wasn't supposed to be promiscuous or vicious. And boy, was I something hateful. I mean, if somebody wronged me, they were cut off. That was probably after I did something very terrible to hurt them or their feelings in return. I couldn't wait to get revenge on people that hurt me. How dare they violate me? I had to get them back. I was never really physical, but I knew how to hit people where it hurt the most, mentally and emotionally. I knew I had the power to hurt people on the inside, and I would do it just because I could. That's what Scorpios do— they sting.

The fact that Scorpio is supposedly known as "the sex sign" gave me an excuse to keep fornicating after I lost my virginity. I figured God knew that I was going to be born under that sign, so He already knew my struggle. Not to mention, I thought I had a strategy. As long as I asked for forgiveness every now and then, God would protect me. As much as I exemplified the positive attributes of being intuitive, loyal, love hard, etc., I was also extremely bad when things went sour. I knew how to play both sides really well. Unfortunately, that wasn't the person God called me to be.

All of those negative characteristics didn't mirror the Spirit I had living inside of me. Galatians 2:22-23 says, "But the fruit of the Spirit is love, joy, peace, forbearance, kindness, goodness, faithfulness, gentleness and self-control. Against such things there is no law." By continuing to fit myself into that mold, I was hindering my ability to change. If I was going to pursue God's purpose for my life, I was going to have to let go of all of the junk that wasn't like Him. No longer could I make the excuse for my behavior and claim that it was acceptable because of my sign. With God's Spirit in me,

I was supposed to become more like Him, not like some made up characters regulated by the stars.

The standards of astrology are not the standards of God; not in our relationships, not in our daily walks, not ever. When we look at Isaiah 47:13-14 it says, "All the counsel you have received has only worn you out! Let your astrologers come forward, those stargazers who make predictions month by month, let them save you from what is coming upon you." No matter what I was going through or what my horoscope said, the stars couldn't save me; only the Spirit of God could. Astrology kept me in spiritual bondage, and I wasn't even aware of it. Why in the world would I want to abide by some prediction that was given to the millions of other people in the world? God's plans for me are specific to just me. Instead of horoscopes, I started calling them horror-scopes because they were keeping my heart and mind away from the thoughts of God. When I'm in need, I surely don't pray to the god of Scorpio, so I definitely shouldn't have been looking to a constellation for direction in my life. My sign couldn't save me from my sin. My sign couldn't speak to my heart. The only thing my sign did was intoxicate my mind and spirit.

In the second chapter of Daniel, King Nebuchadnezzar starts to have dreams and they are disturbing to his sleep. He summons magicians, sorcerers, and astrologers to help him make sense of the visions he's having. The only thing is, he wanted them to tell him what he had dreamed and then interpret it. They wanted him to tell his servants the dream first and then they would interpret it. When you get down to verses ten and eleven it reads, "The astrologers answered the king, there is no one on earth who can do what the king asks! No king, however great and mighty, has ever asked such a thing of any magician or enchanter or astrologer. What the king asks is too difficult. No one can reveal it to the king except the gods, and they do not live among humans."

A human operating outside of the Holy Spirit cannot reveal the plans that God has for you life. God may send you signs of confirmation for what He has already revealed to you, but that's it. All of these fortune tellers, false prophets, and such are merely distractions to God's plans, and should have no say in your life. Your days should be spent pursuing God, not by trying to prove some false prediction that's been given to millions of others. I stopped following Scorpio related tweets on Twitter, I stopped trying to pursue men with signs that were supposedly the most compatible with mine, and just disconnected with it altogether. I still have my tattoo, but it doesn't have the same meaning as before. I got it as a confirmation of who I was at the time. Now it's just a reminder of who I'm not, and what I've overcome. Do I still share traits of my friends that were born around the same time? Sure, but I also share similar traits with other people that were not born under my sign. So I just attribute our similarities to sharing the same Spirit, and not the same constellation. Once I ruled out my astrological sign's ability to give me a sense of purpose, I moved on to the next thing: my Myers-Briggs results.

I was first introduced to the Myers-Briggs Type Indicator during my freshman year of college. I was enrolled in a course called Elon 101, which was supposed to help us get acclimated to college life, and help us discover who we were and what academic path we were going to take. The results of the test give you a ton of different professions you could choose to pursue based on your personality type. The results are 16 different types made up of some combination of the following: introversion (I) or extroversion (E), intuition (N) or sensing (S), feeling (F) or thinking (T), and perception (P) or judging (J)[2].

My results were INTJ, and suggested that I would do well in a field of the sciences, law, business administration, technology, or teaching[3]. Gee, thanks. I had all of those options and still no real sense of purpose. It was nice to know that I had so many options, but that still didn't tell me what I was supposed to be doing or what God's plans were. At the very least, my initial major of pre-med and my final declared major of psychology fell somewhere along a very broad spectrum. My decision to pursue a master's degree in human resource management was a combination of the fact that I would supposedly do well in business administration, and my background in psychology. God didn't tell me to do it, and I hadn't asked him. Thankfully, because He is a loving and faithful God, He still got me through the program. Once I completed my degree, I came to a roadblock. Although I loved what I was doing, I still always felt like something was missing. It seemed like I was supposed to be doing more than just going into work everyday, completing assignments, and collecting a paycheck. Don't get me wrong, my job definitely serves its purpose; however, I just felt incomplete. I couldn't quite put my finger on what it was. Maybe I was supposed to be working at another company or maybe I just needed a different outlook about where I was. Maybe I had chosen the wrong career path altogether. All of the questions that I had and the void I needed filled weren't going to be settled by the results of some personality test. I was running out of options.

After my astrological sign and the Myers-Brigg failed me, I turned to my spiritual gifts assessment results. As part of the new members' class at my church, we are encouraged to take a spiritual gift assessment. The purpose of the test is to help members find their place in ministry. Although we may not all be called to pastor, we are all blessed with different gifts that are to be used to advance the Kingdom of God. No gift is better than the other, as they are all of the same Spirit. While the below list is not all-inclusive, the apostle Paul talks about a number of spiritual gifts and roles in several chapters of the New Testament:

- Romans 12:6-8—perceiver, server, teacher, exhorter, giver, administrator, and compassion person.
- 1 Corinthians 12:7-10—word of wisdom, word of knowledge, faith, gifts of healings, working of miracles,

prophecy, discerning spirits, various kinds of tongues, and interpretation of tongues.

- 1 Corinthians 12:28—apostle, prophet, teacher, miracles, kinds of healings, helps, administration, and tongues.
- Ephesians 4:11—the apostle, the prophet, the evangelist, the pastor, and the teacher.

I first took the assessment the year I rejoined church. I had no idea what spiritual gifts were or that I had them. I have to be honest; the first time I took it I tried to cheat! I thought that if I answered all of the questions just right that I would end up with a gift pertaining to the music ministry. Don't judge me! I was just getting back into church, the thought really scared me in a way, and I wanted the results to be something that I already enjoyed doing. I really enjoyed singing and dancing, so naturally I wanted a gift in the arts. I later came to the realization that I wasn't supposed to pick my spiritual gifts; God had already picked them for me.

Can you imagine if babies somehow had a switchboard inside of the embryo that they could control to select all of their features? Let's see, I think I want blonde hair, green eyes, fair skin, a few freckles, but not too many, and whatever else. The problem with that is that they may not resemble the parents from which they were formed. Paternity test requests would probably skyrocket! How else would you be able to trace a blonde haired, green-eyed baby back to his/

her biological Asian parents? The thought of it even sounds strange.

I can't tell you how many people say I look exactly like my father. I didn't get to pick the features that I wanted to be similar; they were picked for me based on biological formations through the sharing of genes. If God made identification that easy in the natural, how much more do you think He desires for us to look just like Him in the spiritual? God operates in the same way. He gives us features that will allow the world to identify us with Him. People ought to say, "You must be a child of God," based on the fruit of the Spirit that's inside of us.

Why aren't we able to pick our spiritual gifts? I think we would probably pick something that is relatively easy and comfortable to us, and then try to take all of the credit for it. Instead, God gives us specific gifts that may appear unlikely and unfamiliar to us so that when we excel in them, He's the one that gets the glory out of it.

Let's look at the story of Moses. God tells Moses that He wants him to go to Pharaoh and tell him to release the children of Israel. In Exodus 4, Moses pleads to God to send someone else to complete the task because he doesn't speak well. Why would God assign that job to someone with a speech impediment? God can't be that cruel can he? No. God didn't need Moses to be perfect; He just needed him to be willing. Through Moses' weakness, God's power was able to be seen. So if the gifts that God has given you aren't exactly what you would have chosen, know that He has a greater purpose in mind. Trust him; He knows what He's doing.

Even after attempting to cheat, my spiritual gift was not in the gift of the arts. I don't even remember what the initial results were because a couple of months later, I took the test again, without cheating. The results were word of wisdom, service, and administration. What in the world was I supposed to do with that? Surely, I was in no position to be giving someone spirit-led wisdom. I barely knew how to follow the Holy Spirit for myself! With service, I was pretty selective in who I wanted to serve at the time, so that probably wouldn't have been a good idea. With administration, I felt I was too new to be in charge of or leading anything. I read about all of the different ministries that I could join, folded the paper, and put it away. I still had no clue what I was supposed to be doing. I decided to step down from the praise team because I didn't want to keep pretending that God had put me there when in fact He hadn't. For the next few years, I just kind of helped out wherever I saw fit at the time, hoping that at some point I would end up right where God wanted me to be.

After a few years of wandering, things finally started to come together. I didn't exactly know how God was going to use my gifts, but I just believed that He could and that He would. Even though I finally caught a glimpse of God's plans, I realized that I still had growing to do. The more I walked with Him, the more I realized just how unalike we still were.

I had a better sense of what I was supposed to do, but I still wasn't who I was supposed to be. If I was going to fulfill God's purpose for my life, I was going to have to continue to grow and start to change some things. If you really want to fulfill God's purpose for your life, you're going to have to trust Him and allow Him to transform you. He is the One who made you and the plans that you're supposed to complete. He knows what you need and the person you need to become. Whatever resources you have been relying on to try and discover yourself—astrology, personality tests, opinions of others, etc.,—know that God holds the blueprint for your life. Don't just randomly try to fill a void. If you're unsure of what you're supposed to be doing or where you're supposed to be, go to God and ask for guidance. Study 1 Corinthians 2:6-16, which talks about how the things of God are revealed only by the Spirit of God.

Also, in Jeremiah 33:2-3 it says, "This is what the Lord says, he who made the earth, the Lord who formed it and established it—the Lord is his name: Call to me and I will answer you and tell you great and unsearchable things you do not know." He wants to reveal the plans to you, but you must ask Him to show them to you. Once you do ask, be still and listen. A lot of times, God can't get a word in edgewise because we talk over Him with our own thoughts and desires. He speaks, but we can't hear Him because we won't sit still long enough in silence to listen. How do you expect to hear from God if you're not listening? When you do hear Him, write down what He says. Habakkuk 2:2 (AMP) says, "And the Lord answered me and said, Write the vision and engrave it so plainly upon tablets that everyone who passes may [be able to] read [it easily and quickly] as he hastens by." Sometimes you will need to refer back to your notes to make sure that you heard God correctly and to confirm that you're headed in the right direction. Take a spiritual gift assessment. Check with your church to see if they offer one, or there is one that you can take online for free at website such as www.spiritualgiftstest.com. According to their site, if you're new in your walk with Christ, it is recommended that you take the youth assessment rather than the adult assessment, which is for more seasoned Christians. No matter the results, go to God in prayer and ask Him for guidance. Remember, God doesn't need you to be perfect for the job; He wants you to be willing to do the job. Instead of waiting until I had it all together to pursue Him and His plans, I allowed God to change me along the way. A butterfly egg doesn't hatch a butterfly; it hatches a caterpillar that must undergo change. Likewise, in order to fulfill God's purpose for your life, you, too, will have to undergo change. If God has revealed to you the plans for your life, and you have chosen to pursue your destiny, congratulations! The new life inside of you is ready to hatch and now it's time to go on a feeding frenzy!

PREPARING FOR FLIGHT

- What resources have you used to try to discover the purpose for your life? Have they been effective?
- What gifts and talents to you have? How does God want you to use them to minister to others?
- If you are currently serving in ministry, are you serving where God has placed you or where you have placed yourself?
- If you aren't serving in a ministry, why not?
- What were the results of your spiritual gifts assessment? Were you surprised?

Let us pray:

> Lord, I thank you for the gift of your Holy Spirit that is able to reveal all things made mystery to man. Forgive me for seeking knowledge and wisdom from anything that does not represent you. Speak to my heart Lord, and reveal to me the plans that you have created just for me. I thank you for the spiritual gifts that you have entrusted to me. May I use them to bring you glory. Today I choose to lay down my desires and pursue you with my whole heart. It's in Jesus' name that I pray, Amen.

STAGE TWO

The Caterpillar

CHAPTER FIVE

It's Time to Eat!

Then Jesus declared, "I am the bread of life. Whoever comes to me will never go hungry, and whoever believes in me will never be thirsty.

—John 6:35, NIV

Now that your new spirit has hatched, this is where real growth begins. Once hatched, the caterpillar begins what is called a larval state. The Latin origin of larval, which means mask, was a name given to insects during the phase in which their adult form is still hidden[1]. Although the butterfly's egg has hatched, it is not yet a butterfly. Even though you've accepted God's calling, you still have some growing to do. You're on the right track, but you're not yet the person that God has called you to be. God's transformation is not instantaneous, but rather it's a process that takes time. While you're moving towards your destiny, there are changes that need to occur in order to prepare you for flight. God will not release you until He knows that you are ready. Your heart needs to be rooted in God's Word and you will need to put away the things that used to keep you from Him. During this phase the caterpillar spends most of its time eating, shedding, growing, and storing up energy for metamorphosis [2]. Now that you've allowed your spirit to hatch, it's time to eat! You've got a lot of growing to do!

A newborn doesn't know what it needs, but his/her parents are supposed to fill in the gap on their behalf. The parents are responsible for teaching them right from wrong, and establishing a foundation by which they are to live. A newborn doesn't know that there are consequences and rewards based on actions. He/she is supposed to wear clothes, needs to be bathed, etc., and must be taught those things. A baby might cry because it's hungry, but it doesn't know what it needs to eat in order to satisfy the craving. The mother knows that it needs milk, and provides the proper food for the baby. Guess what? You're not a baby anymore! You are now responsible for feeding the spirit that's inside of you. If nobody has to tell you to get dressed everyday, then nobody should have to tell you to read your Bible. Your spirit should be mature enough to know better.

For some of you, your spirit is hungry and you don't know how to satisfy its craving. John 6:35 is very clear about what you need to stay full. You need Jesus! But you have to go to Him to get your meals. Jesus didn't say whoever I go to will never go hungry or thirsty; He said whoever COMES to Him will never go hungry or thirsty. Have you been reading and studying His word or have you been starving your spirit? We've gotten so lazy, and we expect other people to give us a word. We just wait, and wait, hoping that a word will find us, when the Word tells us to come and get it.

During the months of preparation before speaking at the 2012 Daughters by Design conference, I asked God to give me some kind of word to help get over my fears. He led me to a sermon titled "You're Never Really Ready," that was preached by Pastor Steven Furtick of Elevation Church in Charlotte, North Carolina. He was actually preaching at the 2012 Hillsong Conference in Australia at the time. Of course, the title caught my attention right from the beginning because I had been thinking to myself that I wasn't sure I was ready to speak at a women's conference. I had only completed about ten or so five-minute speeches in my Toastmasters club up until that point, and I was supposed to speak for a minimum of thirty minutes. Not to mention, I didn't feel like I was old enough to speak to an audience of women that were mostly older than I was. When I found that sermon I said, "Ok, God. You must have heard me."

Pastor Steven started out the sermon with a reference to Jeremiah chapter 1. I wasn't really familiar with the passage, and as I continued to listen, he came upon verses six through eight, "Alas, Sovereign Lord," I said, "I do not know how to speak; I am too young." But the Lord said to me, "Do not say, 'I am too young.' You must go to everyone I send you to and say whatever I command you. Do not be afraid of them, for I am with you and will rescue you," declares the Lord." Wow! God definitely had my attention, and I felt like He was talking directly to me. He went on and the three points of his sermon were: cancel the audition; you've already got the part, get ready on the way, and stay behind the guide. After I heard that, I was so excited, and I just knew that was the word that I needed to prepare me for the conference.

The next day, I listened to the sermon again. I had heard it the first time, but it still hadn't taken root in my spirit, because I was still a little fearful. The third day, I went to his website to find the sermon and it wasn't there. I literally started to panic. In my mind I'm going, "No, that's my word, I need to hear my word, and I know it was just here yesterday, where did it go?" I couldn't find it, and my heart sank. I didn't stay down for long. I was determined to listen to my word, so thank God for Google! I typed in the sermon title in the search box, and there it was. I found it on another website. After I calmed down and got over the shock of possibly not being able to hear "my" word, I listened to it again. I must have listened to that same sermon for a week straight. I didn't care. God had heard me, He provided, and I was determined to root my spirit in that Word.

For the first time, I realized that I had never been so hungry for God like that in my entire life. I was willing to stop at nothing to feed my spirit. Honestly, that's how we should be on a daily basis. Just as much as we find a way to feed our physical bodies everyday, we need to find a way to feed our spirits everyday. You don't always need a move of God, sometimes you just need to get up and eat!

When I get hungry, my mood starts to change. I get irritable, cranky, short-tempered, and it's not pleasant at all. If I go too long without eating, then my body just starts to shut down altogether. My stomach starts cramping, I get a headache, I start feeling dizzy, and literally get physically sick. That actually happened not too long ago. I was hanging with some friends, we had a full day planned, and I barely ate anything for breakfast. I'm used to eating about six small meals a day, so I was beyond off my eating schedule. By the time we sat down for dinner my head was pounding, I was nauseous, and just felt awful. I tried drinking ginger ale, water, caffeine, and nothing was helping. I asked the waitress if she could bring me some crackers, and she offered to bring me bread. I told her that was fine, and within ten minutes of me eating the bread, my body started to get its life back. My headache subsided, I was back to laughing and joking with the girls, and it was as if nothing had ever happened.

The Word of God is the bread that gives your spirit life. When you don't feed your spirit, its mood starts to change. Negative feelings that you know didn't come from God start popping up, and instead of eating you just let your spirit starve. The caterpillar spends most of this stage eating because it's storing up energy needed for transformation.

Just like you will only last for so long on an empty stomach, you will only last for so long walking around with an empty spirit. You have to be intentional about feeding your spirit. Stop walking around hungry and malnourished. If you're not eating, you're not preparing for change. You will need spiritual strength in order to fulfill God's purpose for your life. If you are going to grow and become who God has called you to be, you're going to have to eat!

When we look at 1 Kings 19, Elijah finds himself in the wilderness while running from the Israelites because he's fearful that they're going to kill him. Once he gets there, he prays that God would take his life and falls asleep under a bush. In verses five through eight, we learn that an angel of the Lord appears to Elijah and tells him to get up and eat. He awakens, finds hot bread and water, eats, and lies back down. The angel appears again with the same message, Elijah eats again, his strength is renewed, and he eventually goes on to carry out the instructions of the Lord. What we see here is that one of God's children is in distress, he calls out to God, and his response is to get up and eat. The bread and the water had already been prepared for Elijah, but he had the choice to eat and drink what was provided for him. God knows and sees what you're going through, and he hears your prayers. He's already told you that you'll never go hungry or thirsty, but you have a choice whether you're going to eat what he's already prepared for you. His word is the bread and water that you need to fill our spirit. Are you going to get up and eat, or are you going to just lie there in your misery, pain, guilt, sin, or whatever else? Whatever you're going through, it's time to move past it; but you're going to have to feed on God's Word in order to do it. That one sermon filled my spirit and remained in me for over a month. God knew what I needed, he led me to the food, but I had to choose whether or not I was going feed it to my spirit. I did, and I still remember it to this day.

I'm telling you, if you're going to fulfill God's purpose for your life you're going to have to feed on His Word like your life depends on it, because it does. When the caterpillar hatches, one of its first meals is the egg from which it came[3]. Then it continues to feed on its host leaf until it's ready for the next phase. God is the host, and His Spirit was planted in your heart, the host leaf. Your spirit is feeding off of whatever is in your heart, as previously discussed referencing Proverbs 4:23. Your spiritual growth depends heavily on your spiritual diet.

Many say that breakfast is the most important meal of the day; so while you're feeding your natural body, you can also feed your spirit. Sign up for an online devotional that will send you daily e-mails or read a bible verse in the morning and apply it to your life. Technology has made it so easy for us to stay in contact with God and his Word on the go. By no means are quick studies replacements for spending quality time with God; but you should put something in your system to jump start your day.

Before I even get out of bed, I've read at least two devotionals, studied at least three scriptures, and prayed. I just have this desire to start my day with God first in order to fill my spirit throughout the day. After that, I may pick random worship songs to sing while I'm getting ready. I drive to work every day in silence. No radio, just me and God. I want to be prepared for whatever lies ahead for that day. If I happen to get out of sorts at some point during the day, I can go to an app on my phone, pull up the bible online, pray, or start singing to get me back to where I need to be spiritually. You're going to have to be intentional about this process and fight through some tough moments. You might be having a hectic day at work, relationship issues, or whatever, and you need to recognize when it's time to refuel on the Word of God. If we can sing songs about getting a refill of some human's love, then surely we can be intentional about getting a refill of the word of God!

Now, for some of you, you're doing a whole lot of eating, but unfortunately you're eating things that are poisoning your spirit, and you may not even realize it. This is definitely a time for you to check your diet. What kind of music do you listen to? What are you watching on TV? What kind of books are you reading? What types of movies are you watching? Some of the things poisoning your spirit may not even be secular, but rather poor theology. All of these things can impact you.

You simply cannot grow in the things of God if you constantly choose to feed off the things of the world. I used to sit and watch all of these different talent shows and reality TV shows for hours every single week. One day I realized that I was spending so much time watching other people go after their dreams that I was missing out on the opportunity to go after my own. I started adding up the number of hours that I spent watching TV every week, and then thought about how much closer to my destiny I would have been had I used that time towards fulfilling my purpose. After that realization, I chose to turn off the TV and spend more time with God. I may have gone from watching about twenty hours of TV a week down to about two. Spending time with God was just that important to me.

Understand that you're not investing in yourself when you sit and watch TV. You're investing in whatever cable or subscription service company you're paying, you're investing in the actors that you're watching, and the networks that you're supporting. I know you've been working all day, and now you're tired, so you don't see any harm in just relaxing and watching a little television. I get that. However, if you're not where God has called you to be, you honestly don't have time to sit and watch TV. I'm simply talking about priorities here. I can either spend my evenings wasting time or I could actually do something productive.

For those of you with jobs, unless you are in a position to quit, there is going to be some overlap for a while until you move past where you are. The key is you have to get moving and start planting some seeds. If you're unhappy with your current circumstances or you desire more, then you're going to have to do the best you can with what you have. You may only have 3 hours in the evening before you're ready to go to bed—use those three hours pursuing your destiny. Whether it's studying your word, working on a business plan, working on your budget, do something to move you closer towards your destiny. Watching TV surely isn't going to get you there.

For those of you that don't watch TV, you still need to identify what it is that's standing in between you and God and remove it. I turned my weekend "free" time in God-time. I thought I deserved to just sit around and do nothing because I had worked all week, but that wasn't bringing me any closer to my destiny. The point is, you're going to have to change something, and really fight through this. The more battles you win, the more fight you will have in you. Keep in the front of your mind that these are temporary sacrifices that will award you long term gains.

Once I realized and truly believed that God had something greater for me than what I could give myself, TV didn't matter. I was more concerned about fulfilling the will of God than anything else. I didn't mind turning off the TV to spend time with God. If I missed a show, so what; I probably wouldn't have remembered the episode in a couple of days, anyway. Besides, none of those people are helping me progress towards my destiny. None of those people have promised to give me hope and a future. None of those people died on a cross for me. We sing these songs like "I give Myself

Away," "I Surrender All," and "My Life is In Your Hands," but then our actions say the opposite. How can we tell God that we give ourselves away, but yet everything else still takes priority over Him? We don't stop cursing, fornicating, or supporting shows that dishonor Him. We won't get out of debt, we don't pursue the calling that He has for our lives, but yet we supposedly give ourselves away to be used by Him. He tells us that if we come to Him we will never go hungry or thirsty, but yet we're satisfied eating the empty calories that the world offers to us on a regular basis. Just because it's on TV or on the radio, it doesn't mean that you have to watch or listen to it. Again, you're old enough to feed yourself. You choose whether or not you're going to fill your spirit with substance or junk.

Also, pay attention to what you're being fed at church. If every sermon you hear only talks about what you can get from God and not what your role is to Him, then your spirit is not getting everything that it needs. Yes, God is a healer, provider, and all of these wonderful things, but what are we to Him? We are supposed to be ambassadors for Christ. If you aren't learning about how your life is supposed to reflect the life of Christ, your growth will be limited. It's almost like eating a cracker and hoping that it'll turn into a 4 course meal by the time it reaches your stomach; that just isn't so! Christianity is a two-way street. Not only do I want to know that I can go to God for whatever I need, but I also want Him to know that He can come to me for whatever He needs. So make sure you are feeding on and being fed all aspects of the Bible and not just a select few topics.

There are things that we are supposed to do for God, and there are things that He promises to do for us. You're going to need more than just a word on prosperity to get you through the transformation process and beyond. If you look at Ephesians 6:10-17, no where in the listing of armor do you see prosperity mentioned. While prospering is great, it won't do much for you in the midst of your tests and battles. So make sure that you're sitting under well-balanced teaching, and that you're really being prepared for your transformation.

This is the time to check your spiritual diet. In whatever areas you need to grow, you should be on a feeding frenzy. Whether it's your finances, relationships, faith, purity, redemption, righteousness, etc., get in your word. I was able to get out of debt by feeding on God's word in the area of stewardship and applying it to my life. You can get your meals directly from Scripture, from books, blogs, devotionals, etc. You have more than enough options. In this phase you're going to need to eat, grow, keep eating, and keep growing. Remember that the rate of your growth is dependent upon your eating. If you need to make some changes to your diet, then do it. Turn off the TV, turn off the radio, put down books that don't glorify God, whatever it is that is poisoning your spirit rather than nourishing it. God knows what your spirit needs, and will have your meal waiting for you when you go to him.

PREPARING FOR FLIGHT

- What is your current spiritual diet? How often are you feeding on God's word?
- In what ways can you keep in touch with God on a regular basis? Through e-mail, internet, apps, etc?
- What are some of the things that are poisoning your spirit?
- What areas in your life do you need to study in order to grow with God?

Let us pray:

> Lord, I thank you for your Word. I believe that with you I will never go hungry or thirsty. Help me to grow, so that I may become more like you. Give me the strength to remove those things that are harmful to my spirit. Break down the barriers that stand between you and me so that I may pursue my purpose wholeheartedly. Today I give the desires of my flesh away so that I can be used by you, Lord. It's in Jesus' name that I pray. Amen.

CHAPTER SIX

Focus on Your Leaf

Do you not know that in a race all the runners run,
but only one gets the prize? Run in such a way as
to get the prize.

—1 Corinthians 9:24, NIV

Caterpillars will typically only eat the leaves of the plant on which their mother specifically chose to lay her eggs[1]. Each species has a specific diet, and they don't tend to jump around from plant to plant trying to test out which leaves taste better before they start eating. They trust that the leaf on which they hatched was picked with intent, and they immediately start to consume its contents. Likewise, the gifts that God placed inside of you were hand-picked specifically for you. That doesn't mean that you get to keep them for yourself; there is a greater purpose behind your gifts. He knows your capabilities and your deficiencies, but He still chose you in spite of. You can try to run from your gifts, change them, etc., but the will of God always outlasts even our greatest insecurities. So no matter how many times you try to get away, somehow you will find yourself right back where He wanted you.

When we look at the story of Jonah, God gave Jonah an assignment to go preach against the city of Nineveh because of their wickedness. Instead of doing what God told him to do, he ran away, hopped on a boat, and sailed out to sea. Sometimes the purpose God gives us may not be thrilling to us and may even scare us. But by running away, Jonah not only put himself at risk, he put the sailors at risk, as well as the city of Nineveh. The purpose that God gives you isn't just about you. He wants to use you as a vessel for a greater purpose. So, whenever we make the choice to do anything other than obey God, we put other people's lives and possibly their souls at risk. Somebody's life is depending on us whether we respond to the call or not. Even though Jonah disobeyed God, his assignment to save the city of Nineveh remained the same. However, he had to make the choice to fulfill his purpose. Even though Jonah ran away from God, God went after him. He gets Jonah's attention by sending a violent storm and a big fish to swallow him after he was thrown off the boat.

Do you ever feel like God is trying to get your attention? You know He has placed a calling on your life but instead you continue to pursue other things. The promotion that you wanted didn't come through, that relationship wasn't what you hoped, your business plan isn't coming together, etc. God is not trying to harm you; He's trying to get you to come back towards Him. He's placed a specific calling on your life on purpose, but unlike the caterpillar, you're out there trying to taste and pursue other plants. Jonah spent three days and three nights in the belly of the fish. It was during that time that he reconciled with God, and surrendered to His calling. If you feel like God is trying to get your attention, take a time out and spend time with Him. Acknowledge how faithful He has been to you in spite of your disobedience, and then commit to His ways. As God continues to reveal His purpose for your life, continue to feed on the resources that He gives you. Continue to learn more about Him, study your spiritual gifts, and just seek God with your whole heart. Somebody is depending on you to fulfill your purpose. Just because you don't do it, it doesn't mean that somebody else will or that it will eventually disappear. Your assignment belongs to you.

Sometimes I wonder how many opportunities I missed to impact someone's life because I wasn't where God needed me to be. I know that we can often recite Philippians 4:13 (NKJV), "I can do all things through Christ who strengthens me," when it pertains to getting through times of trouble, but can we also apply it to pursuing God's purpose for our lives? To be able to completely surrender and say, "Lord, I don't know why you want me to do this or how you're going to use me, but I know that I will make it because you are with me." A statement of that caliber may be hard to grasp at first, but as you continue to study God's word and spend time with him, you will learn to trust Him. You will come to know His Word as being true and you will be able to apply it to your life in ways that were once unseen. Your faith and obedience are going to get you to your destiny—that's it. It may not sound like a lot, but it's more than enough. I know you may not be able to see more than a footstep in front you, but as long as it's God's footprint, you will be ok. Believe me, the moment he doesn't hear your footsteps behind His, He's going to turn around and come looking for you. He loves you so much and wants the world to be able to recognize that you are His. Focus on preparing your heart for the journey ahead instead of trying to run away from it.

Sometimes you may not run away, but you can also be drawn away by other distractions. Inevitably, now that you're pursuing the things of God, you will start to notice temptations from the things that you're trying to outgrow. You'll get invitations to places you no longer desire to visit, phone calls or texts from people that belong in your past, offers for products that you should no longer consume, new TV shows, and a host of other opportunities that the devil will use to try to distract you from pursuing God. On the one hand, you must recognize who is doing the tempting. God is not tempting you; it's the enemy. How do we know? James 1:13 says, "When tempted, no one should say, "God is tempting me." For God cannot be tempted by evil, nor does He tempt anyone."

However, it is through temptation that we are tested by God. The enemy's goal is to entrap you in sin, while God's goal is to make you strong enough to ward off sin. God's faithfulness is explained in 1 Corinthians 10:13, "No temptation has overtaken you except what is common to mankind. And God is faithful; he will not let you be tempted beyond what you can bear. But when you are tempted, he will also provide a way out so that you can endure it."

If you know that God is calling you away from a potentially harmful situation, person, or thing that is trying to tempt you, simply tell it no. We like to say that it's easier said than done, but that is simply a phrase of defeat. You will have to learn to speak into your victories instead of against them. Remind yourself daily of your progress and that you're not going back from where you came no matter what it takes. Your future is so much larger and brighter than your past. Don't risk it all for a moment of pleasure.

Be mindful that you can be lured into temptation in any area of your life. Whether it's your finances, health, relationships, job, or anything else, you still have the power to resist. I remember when I was about six months away from paying off my last student loan. I could see the end in sight, when the compressor went out in my refrigerator. I had worked so hard and couldn't understand why it was happening to me. The amount that it would cost to replace it with the exact same model was more than I could afford at the time. This model was the one that I had matched perfectly with all of the other appliances in my kitchen and there were features on it that I really liked. I had a choice: to stay within my budget or to satisfy the child-like desires of my flesh. When it came down to it, my commitment to God was more important to me than the aesthetics of an appliance. Not only did I get a replacement that was as close to the original as possible, but I also got it for about $350 less than I was going to have to originally pay for it. This isn't a story about money, but rather it is proof that God rewards obedience and sacrifice. And I mean, my mother and I must have been in the store for at least an hour before I made up my mind. She knew my intentions, and she was there to support me no matter what I decided.

As you pursue God, make sure that you have people in your corner that will be there to support you. You're going to have weak moments, so make sure that you're prepared for battle. Don't think that the devil is going to lie down and watch you pursue your destiny, because he won't. He'll let you make progress, and then attack you when you least expect it. Just as much as the devil can use people to make you fall, God can use people to protect you and push you forward. Really be mindful about who you're hanging around during this process. Ask yourself, are they pushing me towards God or leading me away from Him?

Although I had gotten over one financial hurdle, the battles kept coming. Six months later, after I had paid off my loan and it was time for my car inspection, it failed for several reasons, totaling well over my savings yet again. I remembered how God had come through before and so I sought Him for His help. Like the first time, He came through. About $500 worth of repairs was all completed for about $350 less. While I grew frustrated and angry, I was determined to keep my eyes on God.

After that, I thought I was free and clear from any further issues. Not so; the devil hit me with the biggest blow that I had seen all year. In the dead heat of the summer, my entire air conditioning system had to be replaced. I had been through enough, and I was devastated, embarrassed, and hurt. Everyone knew how hard I had worked to get out of debt, and it seemed like I was the victim of a big joke. As far as I had come, there was no way that I was going back into debt. As hot as it was, I suffered for six weeks without air conditioning. I spent weekends at my parents' house when it was too hot to stay at my own, I bought a box fan, and toughed it out. Some people asked if I was going to take out a loan and suggested using a credit card, but I was willing to sweat in my sleep every night before giving in to the devil. While I was upset about losing the money, the strength and endurance that I built during that time was worth more than what I lost. So the next time the devil rears his ugly head, I can look back at my victories and draw strength and encouragement from them.

If I hadn't resisted the temptation, I wouldn't have the understanding that I have now. I was tempted, but God knew that I could handle it if I just kept my focus on Him. Although it wasn't easy, it wasn't impossible either. As He was there for me at every obstacle I faced, He will be there for you as well. Once the devil saw how resilient I was, he moved on. See, the caterpillar typically has snake-like markings on it designed to ward off predators[2]. As you continue to transform, you begin to develop Christ-like characteristics. Things will start to work out in your favor because the opposition will be distracted by your appearance. They will see that in times of trouble you'll be the one that keeps your composure. Instead of being provoked to react negatively, you can just smile, sit back, and watch God do the heavy lifting for you. If the caterpillar's appearance doesn't keep a predator away, it will soon find out upon attack that the caterpillar has been feeding on leaves that are toxic to its system[2]. One encounter is enough for the predator to learn not to attack the caterpillar in the future. Like so, God's Word is toxic to the enemy. He's been used to you just curling up and letting him win, but not anymore. While he may not think that you're as strong as you are, when he attacks you and gets a taste of God's Word, he'll learn real quickly what he's up against. He may not go down without a fight, but he will eventually go down. The Spirit of God is in you, and the more you feed it, the more powerful it becomes. So, no matter how tough the fight keep your eyes on God, stay in His Word, and allow Him to continue to strengthen and transform your heart.

Not only have I been tested in my finances, but in the area of relationships as well. Psalm 1 tells us that the person who does not walk in the ways of the wicked is blessed; and the person who meditates on God's Word is like a tree planted by streams of water, which will yield fruit in its season. I used to look at other people's relationships and think, well hey, they were out of God's will and they still got married or they're still a happy couple, so I will be fine. The devil has duped us into making sin the status quo. People have sinned for years, and have still survived, succeeded, etc., so what's the big deal? However, I wasn't thinking about God and His will. God's will is left undone when His children do not follow his commands. God's will is left undone when we do not transform into the new creations that He predestined for us. God's will is left undone when our daily walks do not draw others to Christ. God misses out on His glory, and we miss out on our blessings by attempting to gain them before our time and by the ways of the world. But guess what? You don't have to operate the world's way! Your season of reaping is on the horizon, and God wants to lead you every step of the way if you'll let Him be your guide. Fight the temptation to go back from where you came, and cling to God like never before.

As you continue to draw close to God, be aware of getting caught up in other people's destinies. Sometimes we see how God has moved in the lives of our fellow brothers and sisters and expect Him to move the same way in our lives. While He can, you are also unique. God's glory is definitely something to be admired, but don't let it take you off of your course.

You never know what that person had to endure to get to where they are. Although you may witness the evidence of the victory, you may not see the details of the battle or the wounds that it left. You may not be able to handle what that person was built to endure. Every Christian wasn't meant to be a pastor of a megachurch or a national gospel-recording artist. However, God has a special work for you to do that is just as important as the next person's assignment. It doesn't mean that you are any less blessed or anointed; you're simply on a different assignment. He has put something inside of you that is just as great as the next person.

At the end of the day, continue to run your race. Whatever obstacles or hurdles the devil puts in your way, use the power of the Holy Spirit to get you through it. Hebrews 12:1 (NLT) says, "Therefore, since we are surrounded by such a huge crowd of witnesses to the life of faith, let us strip off every weight that slows us down, especially the sin that so easily trips us up. And let us run with endurance the race God has set before us." There are people in the world that are depending on you to fulfill your purpose. The things that you are able to endure will become a living testimony of God's power. People will be watching to see if you're really going to change and if God is really going to use you. As you continue to mature in the ways of God, you will notice that things that used to weigh you down like fear, doubt, uncertainty, and sin will start to lighten. If you're going to fly in your purpose, you aren't going to be able to take everything with you. You will need to lose some things, so that God can replace them with the tools that you need to complete your assignment. While you may not fully understand it, there is a method to what may sometimes seem like utter chaos and madness. Above all else, know in your heart that God is with you and your life is safe in His hands. You have a great future ahead of you and He's going to see you through it. Keep pressing!

PREPARING FOR FLIGHT

- Has God given you a task that you would rather run from than complete? Why are you running?
- How did God attempt to get your attention after you turned away from your assignment?
- Since you've decided to pursue God, in what ways have you been tempted? Were you able to fight them?
- Who in your life is helping to push you closer to God? Who is drawing you further away from him?
- How can you help someone else overcome an obstacle or temptation that they might be facing?

Let us pray:

> Lord, I thank you for the unique assignment that you've given me. Remove any fear and doubt that I may have in my abilities to complete the task at hand. As I continue to pursue you, I pray that when I am tempted that you will come to my rescue. Give me the strength that I need so that I may endure to the end. May my victories inspire others and bring glory to your name. It's in Jesus' name that I pray, Amen.

CHAPTER SEVEN

The Signs of Growth

So all of us who have had that veil removed can see
and reflect the glory of the Lord. And the Lord—who
is the Spirit—makes us more and more like him as
we are changed into his glorious image.
                    —2 Corinthians 3:18, NLT

As a caterpillar grows, it also outgrows its skin, and goes through a series of shedding cycles. The more the caterpillar eats, the more it grows, and the tighter its skin becomes. Once the body realizes that it has run out of room, it begins to molt so that it can release the old skin and prepare to live in its new, brighter, bigger skin[1]. The act of shedding is proof that the caterpillar has been eating and growing.

Likewise, as you continue to study God's Word and grow, you should notice an overall change in your appearance. When someone says, make sure you have a church home where you're "growing," what does that mean? How do I know if I'm growing and what comparison do I have? Am I growing because I'm going to church more than I did before? Am I growing because I've joined a ministry? Am I growing because my lifestyle has changed, or my relationships are getting better? Am I growing because my spirit looks more like God's than my sinful flesh? What does a "grown up" Christian look like? How do you know you're growing? You start to outgrow the skin that you're in. Negative attitudes that used to fit all of a sudden don't fit any more. Bad habits that were once natural all of a sudden feel unnatural. You're pursuing God on a consistent basis. You and others around you start to notice a visible change.

When I finally decided to pursue God's will for my life I knew that some things were going to have to change. I couldn't stay the same and grow into God's image simultaneously. It had to be one or the other. The changes didn't all happen at once, but as I drew closer to God, different layers came off at different times in the process. One of the first things I did was focus on getting my finances in order. I knew that whatever God was calling me to do, that I was going to need to be financially free in order to do it. I prayed that God would show me how to be a better steward, and once he did, I actually started to do the things that he showed me. I grew so much closer to God because he was my biggest motivation. It wasn't about paying off student loans and credit cards so that I could buy more stuff for myself; I wanted to be free to pursue my purpose. I wanted to be free to give when God needed me to. If I was supposed to start a business, I wanted to have the means to do it without having to borrow. Proverbs 22:7 says that "the borrower is slave to the lender," and I knew that God hadn't intended for me to be in financial bondage. That was not His will for my life. As well, I was obstructing my pursuit of Him with the weight of debt pulling on my heart. I was always trying to figure out how I could get more money instead of focusing on how to get more God in my life. Once I focused on Him, everything else started to fall into place.

It wasn't an easy process, and there were no money windfalls, but it was a time of growth and testing. How serious was I about getting out of debt? Did I really trust God? I had to put together a plan and put it to work. I had to retrain the way I thought about money. When I completed the process, poor stewardship became a layer of old skin that I could shed. As a result of my shedding, I started a blog that focuses on biblical stewardship. Not only could I see a change in my own spending, budgeting, saving, sowing, etc, but the world also saw a result of my shedding as well. I felt like I needed to have the image of the Lord in my finances so that I could be a light unto the world. You will have to actively pursue change.

Once I completed that shed, I moved on to the next thing. Please don't think that all of this happened overnight, because it didn't. These changes took place throughout the years after I rejoined church, and are still taking place even today. There were so many directions in which I could have gone, that I just asked God for guidance on how He wanted to transform me. I came upon Psalm 19:14 that says, "May these words of my mouth and this meditation of my heart be pleasing in your sight, Lord, my Rock and my Redeemer," and was immediately convicted. I started to wonder if the words that came out of my mouth were actually pleasing to God. I made the choice right then to stop using curse words. I didn't want to praise God with the same mouth that spewed out foul language. As often as I made the choice to use them, I knew that I could also make the choice not to. I'm not judging anyone that does use curse words; I am just merely saying that where God was taking me, I knew I had to leave it behind. That's not to say that I don't slip up every now and then, but instead of coming out in every other word, they are now few and far in between. I also had to shed my old way of thinking about relationships. After so many ungodly and failed attempts, I committed to learning how to become the woman that God wanted me to be first. I listened to teachings on biblical womanhood, purity, submission, etc. My mindset about dating and things that I desired in a mate had to completely change. God had to remove layer upon layer of filth so that He could create a better me. By no means does the shedding process make you a perfect human being. However, it will break down the barriers that are keeping you from fulfilling the purpose that God has for your life. Whatever it is that you need to shed, whether it's a bad habit, bad relationships, bad thinking, etc. get word on those areas and allow God to renew you.

The molting period can be very stressful for a caterpillar, as it makes it vulnerable to injury and possibly death if disturbed during the process[2]. Understand that as you move forward in the things of God, the devil will try to attack you. You may start to second guess whether or not you're ready to let go, you may allow fear to enter into your spirit, or you may feel like giving up at times. He may try to use the people that are closest to you. Friends and family that used to support you may all of a sudden have negative things to say about your growth. They may not believe that you're serious or that change is even possible for you. Don't fall for it. You must remain focused on the destiny ahead. You must know in your heart that you are being transformed into something bigger and better than you were before you started to shed the things that were keeping you from growing.

During the molting phase, an outsider is unable to see what's taking place underneath. Don't be surprised if someone can't understand what you're going through or if they're unable to see your growth right away. If and when it happens, remember Psalm 118:8, "It is better to take refuge in the Lord than to trust in humans." Both you and God know what's going on, so take a hold of that fact and keep it close to your heart no matter what. They will see the transformation for themselves in due time.

Once you shed the old skin, leave it there! Proverbs 26:11 (NLT) says, "As a dog returns to its vomit, so a fool repeats his foolishness." You shed that skin for a reason; it no longer fits you! I often hear people talk about trying to reopen doors that God closed, and trying to fit back into old skin is just as foolish. I've tried to force bad relationships to work knowing that there was a reason why we broke up in the first place. Each time, I still found myself at a dead end. The sin and negativity that you shed is dead, so stop trying to walk around with a carcass on your back. After a while it's going to start to smell, and it will eventually stink up your spirit! When God removes a person or thing from your life, He does it so that you can move forward. It may seem odd at first, uncomfortable, and maybe even painful, but trust him through the process. You are on your way to becoming something great!

Remaining in old skin will affect both your growth and your spiritual diet. If you don't shed the skin that you're in, you will inhibit your spiritual growth. The whole point of shedding is so that you can grow into your developing spirit. When a caterpillar molts, the new skin is already waiting for him to crawl into it. It doesn't have to sit and contemplate whether or not it wants to grow, its body knows that it has outgrown itself and triggers the new growth. Unlike the caterpillar, you have a choice between growing into the new skin that God is developing for you or staying in your old skin. Ephesians 3:20 says, "Now to him who is able to do immeasurably more than all we ask or imagine, according to his power that is at work within us." Your growth in Christ is only limited by one thing . . . YOU. God is in you, the question is, will you let His power do the work in you? Your sin will suffocate you if you let it. That is why you need to let it go. Not only will it suffocate you, but it will also affect your diet.

At some point, you should grow beyond the stage of receiving word on basic "house rules" such as tithing, purity, forgiveness, etc. You will need to mature to the point of understanding the power of the Spirit of God and how to activate it regarding your life's calling. If you're still debating on whether or not you're going to tithe, wait until marriage to have sex, forgive your neighbor, extend grace to a family member, etc. you will have a difficult time receiving and applying a mature word.

In 1 Corinthians 3:1-3 (NLT) Paul talks about having to feed the believers milk because their sinful nature kept them from being mature enough to receive solid food. Hebrews 5:12-13 (NLT) says, "You have been believers so long now that you ought to be teaching others. Instead, you need someone to teach you again the basic things about God's word. You are like babies who need milk and cannot eat solid food. For someone who lives on milk is still an infant and doesn't know how to do what is right."

If you're going to pursue God's calling for your life, you're going to have to mature in your spiritual diet. You need to be free to focus on tapping into God's power, moving mountains, impacting communities, discipleship, etc. But if you're still wrestling with Christian basics, your spirit will not be ready for solid food, which will impact your growth. As you would not spend your natural adult life drinking milk from a baby bottle, neither should you spend your life drinking spiritual milk. More nutrients are required in order to prepare you for transformation. Remember, the caterpillar is eating so that it can store up enough energy to get him through the next stage. Likewise, you will need more than milk to get you ready for your transformation.

In my own experience, I started to receive the deeper areas of God's word as I cleaned up the bad areas in my life and drew closer to Him. I couldn't have imagined activating God's power or pursuing my calling while trying to hide from God in shame because of sins that I had committed a million and one times. Every time I said I wouldn't do it again, the next day I was right back at it. My own guilt stood in the way of me growing in the word of God. Now don't get me wrong, I still knew who God was, but I wasn't growing in His ways. That isn't God's intention for our lives. Salvation sets us free from sin. Not just in a sense of forgiveness, but also in our urges to commit the offenses. When I finally decided to let that filth go, I could receive God in a more mature way.

It is during the shedding process that Psalm 37:4 took on a new meaning. "Take delight in the Lord, and he will give you the desires of your heart." As I began to transform into His image, my desires started to look like His as well. I used to think that this text meant that I could expect anything that I wanted from God if I told Him that I loved Him enough times, sang a few gospel songs, or had great attendance at church. To me, I was delighting myself in the Lord. In reality I was just checking a few things off of my to-do list and trying to manipulate God.

Have you ever come across someone that was nice to you just because they wanted something? That's exactly what I was doing to God. It wasn't until I actually started to get to know Him that I understood that I was supposed to enjoy His company, and I genuinely did. I didn't just go to Him every time I wanted something, but I just wanted to feel His presence and hear His voice. I just wanted the comfort of knowing that He was here with me. As our relationship deepened, my desires became more selfless than they were before, and I was OK with it. I started to go to Him with more mature requests rather than just begging for forgiveness. I desired His wisdom, His knowledge, and His heart. I could hear Him better, I received revelation on a regular basis, and we just grew closer altogether. His desires became my desires. That is what the Scripture means. So use the spiritual milk to get you beyond the basics, but then as you grow, you should notice that your dietary needs will also change. Yes, there is a lot going on during this stage, but God will be there with you every step of the way!

Your spiritual growth is not just some object of the imagination. You will see the manifestation of transformation in your natural being. Make note of the changes that are taking place. Observe your prayer life, your speech, your behaviors, your attitude, etc. Jot them down in a journal if you have to. You won't have to guess whether or not you're growing. Not only will you see it, but others around you will notice a change as well. If you're unsure, talk to God about it. Ask Him what change would look like in your life, and listen intently. When I'm unsure if I'm growing, I meditate on Psalm 139:23 (KJV) that says, "Search me, O God, and know my heart: try me, and know my thoughts." God will answer, and wants you to know that He's working in you, for you, and through you. He wants to see you fly, and will do whatever it takes to help you reach your destiny. Commit today to allow Him to grow you, feed you, and stretch you, so that you can be prepared for the next phase.

PREPARING FOR FLIGHT

- What are some of the negative things/behaviors that are keeping you from growing spiritually?
- Think about a time that you tried to make a positive change. What were some of the attacks that you encountered and from whom?
- What is something that you've shed and tried to pick back up? Why?
- What are your conversations with God like? In what ways can they mature?
- Have you noticed any changes in your behavior since you've been drawing closer to God? If so, what are they?

Let us pray:

Dear Lord, I thank you for your gift of salvation that allows us to be free from sin. I ask you to remove from me anything that is not like you. Forgive me for when I have fallen short and tried to reopen doors that you closed. Today I desire to grow a deeper relationship with you, and I'm willing to let go of whatever is standing in my way. Lord I ask that you continue to feed me your word, and strengthen me for the days to come. It's in Jesus' name that I pray, Amen.

CHAPTER EIGHT

Caterpillars Can't Fly

To get where you want to go, you first have to become
the person God wants you to be.
—Devon Franklin, Produced by Faith

There are several things that a butterfly can do that a caterpillar can't. A caterpillar doesn't have the physical equipment that it needs to fly, nor is it mature enough to reproduce other caterpillars. These are some of the benefits of reaching adulthood. If a caterpillar wants to be able to do these things, it must first complete the metamorphosis process. Like so, there are plans that God has for you that won't be given to you until you're ready to handle them. Certain jobs, relationships, opportunities, visions, etc. won't be presented to you until you've matured enough to handle the responsibility. You simply cannot rush God. His timing is perfect, and you will only frustrate yourself while trying to cheat or prematurely accelerate the process. A newborn baby develops motor skills over time and eventually they're able to crawl, walk, and then run. Trying to do any of those things without the proper muscle development and strength could result in painful injuries. Likewise, you will need to be patient with God while He is preparing you for your purpose. He knows what you're able to handle based upon the conditions of your heart and the development of His spirit in you. If you attempt to take matters into your own hands, sooner or later you will end up falling short.

God will not give you an executive level assignment while you're operating on entry level qualifications. By that I mean, God will not promote you until your heart is prepared to receive the assignment. We go around chasing all of these things like love, jobs, degrees, fame, money, etc, and not once do we stop, go to God and say, Lord, what is your will? Am I ready for this? Am I on the right path? We think we know what we want and that path that we're supposed to take, but God has something greater in mind. Proverbs 19:21 says, "Many are the plans in a person's heart, but it is the Lord's purpose that prevails." Do you ever sit back and think that the void that you feel or the obstacles that you're facing are the results of being misaligned with God's plans for your life?

We live in a society where we can get things that we want whether we're ready for them or not. In our finances we're able to buy things on credit if we don't have the money at the moment of purchase. In our jobs, sometimes if you know the right people you can be placed in positions that would otherwise be unavailable to you based on your level of experience. In our relationships, people just want to be loved so badly that they'll settle for anyone. In church people want to "look" blessed, instead of just living a blessed life. One day we look up and wonder why our lives are in shambles. The truth is we've taken matters out of the hands of the One who knows all, and have put them into the hands of the ones that think they know it all. God tells us to be still, to be patient, but we let the lives of others, and the glitz and glamour take us out of position instead.

Proverbs 16:32 (NLT) says, "Better to be patient than powerful; better to have self-control than to conquer a city." God will give you His power when you need it, and He also has the ability to give you a city if need be. However, we must first desire to develop His qualities, such as patience and self-control, before desiring to capture material things. "But seek first his kingdom and his righteousness, and all these things will be given to you as well" Matthew 6:33. Do we really believe this scripture? If so, then why aren't we acting like it? God didn't intend for you to go around chasing things; He wants to meet your needs. The thing that He requires is that you seek after Him first with a pure heart and unselfish motives. Even during the spiritual transformation process, the goal isn't to chase after wings and status. The goal is to get closer to God while knowing that by faith He will set us free to fly as a reward for our obedience to Him.

Even though some have said that I'm successful at this point in my life, I've still often found myself wandering and searching for more. Not in a sense of being dissatisfied or ungrateful, but in a sense of being unfulfilled. I've often wondered if I should be pursuing more education, upper level positions, entrepreneurship, etc. I would come up with ideas and then pray that God would make them work. I can't say that I was really pursuing my purpose; but rather I was just willing to take a chance on something other than what I was doing at the time. Things just never quite seemed to come together. It's not that I didn't want them to, but deep down it just didn't feel right.

I've been attempting to write several books for over a year, but I somehow just couldn't get them going. The topics, such as living single or being debt free, were very close to my heart; but I would complete a couple of pages, and then my inspiration would run dry. Once I abandoned one book idea, then I would start another. I tried for months, and still nothing. It wasn't until I asked God what He wanted me to write, that the floodgates opened. What was previously a struggle under my own will suddenly became almost effortless under God's power. I completely surrendered to Him. Each day before I sat down to write, I would ask God to prepare my heart and mind to receive His words, and I would acknowledge that I was merely a transcriber for Him. It's not that I wasn't supposed to be writing, but God had a greater vision in mind for my writing and I finally listened to Him.

There was so much growing that I had to do before I could even get to the point of humbling myself before the Lord. I had to get in His word, develop a relationship with Him, get rid of some bad habits, and mature. Sure, I was ready to accomplish a few goals on my own terms, but in regards to pursuing God's purpose, I wasn't ready. My heart wasn't in the right place. All of the things that I was trying to do were for my own selfish reasons, not God's. He wasn't going to get glory out of any of it because they were things that I could have done on my own, and God knew that. I figured that since we were on "good terms" that He would work miracles through whatever I put my hands to, and that wasn't the case. You simply can't change God's plans. God releases His visions onto us so that the world will see Him, not just our own abilities. Understand that the caterpillar phase is a stage of preparation. Yes you're growing, yes you're making progress, but it is God that releases you to fly on His terms. We have to remember that it is God who prepares plans for us; we don't make plans for Him!

I often hear people talking about making vision boards. I've even made a few in the past. I had all of these material things on there like a house, a nice ring, money, a husband, a nice car, and one thing closely related to God, which was debt freedom. The current visions that you're chasing, whose visions are they exactly? Are they visions that you came up with or visions that God has given you? Sometimes we feel like since we've gotten our faith built up and we're feeling powerful that we can just go do whatever our heart's desire. Maybe you can, but what does God desire? Are you pursuing Him or are you pursuing ideas of the current trends and society? Is God really in control or are you trying to control Him? God wants you to succeed so badly that He's willing to put in the time and effort to get you ready for your calling. He doesn't want to throw you out into the deep end and leave you there to figure it out on your own. He wants to develop you, guide you, provide for you, and cheer you on. But you have to be patient enough to allow God to give you your wings, instead of trying to put them on yourself. If you're going to pursue your purpose, you will have to allow God to interrupt your plans.

The same goes for relationships. Caterpillars don't mate with other caterpillars. Not only are they unequipped, but they aren't mature enough. We have so many caterpillars mating all over this world and wonder why we end up with households full of immature believers. You need to be focused on becoming who God has called you to be before worrying about finding a mate. For those of you that are already married, it's not too late; you can still find out how you can develop and expand God's Kingdom together.

I can only imagine how much different a relationship is when both people already know who they are in Christ; to find someone to support their purpose and to pursue God in tandem. I know that relationships aren't perfect and they require work, but the last thing you need is two people together that are lost and confused about the direction in which their life is going. How will you be able to assist your mate if you're unaware of your own identity? You can't help your mate if you're so distracted with trying to find yourself. If one of you finally figures it out, then all of a sudden you don't know each other anymore or the other person may have a totally different plan in mind. How can you be mad at your mate when you didn't know who you were when you got together? It just seems like so many people have no idea why they're here on this earth other than to work a job, get married, reproduce, pursue riches, etc. When it comes to finding a mate, they hook up with someone that's just as lost as they are and hope that they're able to find their way through life together. Come on. There has to be so much more to life than that. Yes, I am aware that people continue to grow and people change, but you should at least be sharing the same roadmap!

Before I really understood who God called me to be, my "requirements" in a mate were completely different. I just wanted someone that met a certain height requirement, was saved, financially stable, attractive, and all of these other surface level type of things. I wasn't thinking about whether or not God's plans for our lives were compatible. But now, I'm expecting to be found by someone that's going to be my partner on purpose and with purpose.

We see in Genesis 2 that Adam had a God-given purpose before Eve came along. Then God created Eve with a purpose of helping Adam. The two of them together were then supposed to work in tandem fulfilling their assigned duties. So not only do I need to know my purpose, but my mate does as well so that we can fulfill our duties effectively. Point blank, however God plans to use you, the ultimate goal behind it will be to serve others and to draw others to Him. You and your mate should have an understanding of what that's going to look like up front so that you can help each other accomplish God's will. So I'm expecting to be in a relationship with another butterfly, as should you. Just be patient for your transformation, because once you become a butterfly you'll have a much better view, unlike when you're a caterpillar inching along the ground.

Also understand that there is a testimony waiting to be birthed out of your transformation. The butterfly gives us visual proof that it has survived metamorphosis. It has something to show for its obedience and surrender to the process. Think about everyone that you would be able to inspire, not just with your words, but with your works. Your transformation is proof that God's word is true and living. That He still turns messes into messages for the world even today.

I often feel like there aren't enough butterflies here on earth. There are plenty of caterpillars trying to act the part, but their actions say something completely different. So many Christians claim they can fly, but when the time comes, the results look more like a failure to launch. It's kind of like the fig tree mentioned in Mark 11:13. The tree had the appearance of having fruit because of its leaves, but once Jesus walked up to it, he found that there were no figs on it. It wasn't the season for figs. At some point, God's children have to get in season and produce fruit from the Lord. People in church appear to be in full bloom, but then when the world gets close to us, they don't see God. It is almost like the old bait and switch trick. We have to be mindful that the fruit of His spirit is never out of season.

For the longest time I never wanted to invite anyone to church because there was nothing to see but a bunch of caterpillars, including myself, and maybe a handful of butterflies. I don't just mean caterpillars that were newly hatched, but I'm talking about five, ten, fifteen, twenty plus year old caterpillars. There was no transformation; so if God wasn't working in us, then I definitely didn't think that I could sell His abilities to anyone I brought to church with me. But the good news was, I had a choice. I could either stay in spiritual infancy, or I could continue on with the process and let God have his way with me. I think people go to churches hoping to find a butterfly garden, but instead they find a bunch of aged butterfly eggs and caterpillars. Where's the transformation? God needs you to transform so that He can take you to new heights. In order to fulfill the calling that is on your life you're going to have to let God work in you, remove some things, and develop you into a brand new creature. You might be able to play the part, but you can't reproduce what you don't have.

I say all of that to say, be honest with yourself. If you're still a caterpillar, then do what you need to do in order to move forward in the process. There is still so much more in store for you. God still wants to grow a deeper relationship with you and get you ready for flight. Just remember that you can't rush the process. Be still for a minute, pour out your heart to God, and ask Him to order your steps. I'm not saying that God can't, and won't use you where you are, but I am saying that you need to confirm your positioning and timing with Him. If God is truly Lord over your life, then you should be consulting Him on a regular basis as it pertains to every area of your being. Psalm 127:1 says "Unless the Lord builds the house, the builders labor in vain." Why continue to work so hard for something that doesn't glorify the Lord? I would rather know that my labor has more purpose than a paycheck that barely meets my needs and that God is with me every step of the way.

You shouldn't have to force God's purpose to come into fruition. You will have to do the work for it, but it shouldn't feel forced. If something in your life isn't getting off the ground, seek God. Perhaps you're trying to fly and God wants you to hold off for just a little while longer or there's still some extra baggage that you need to lose. Maybe He is waiting on you to take that first step of faith. If you're single, continue to let God shape you. Feed on His word, shed those layers of filth, and get ready for transformation. Let Him lead you to the butterfly that is supposed to be in your life. If you're married, maybe you need to have what I like to call "a come to Jesus" session. Ask God how He can use your marriage for ministry. You may even start by simply ministering to each other first. God wants to see you fulfill your purpose in this life, but He requires your heart and your patience. Whatever you do, just don't stop here. Continue to seek God, look for His cues, and keep your eyes on your destiny. You're so much closer than you think you are!

PREPARING FOR FLIGHT

- The visions, goals, and dreams that you're pursuing, do they belong to God or do they belong to you?
- Have you attempted to pursue something like a job, relationship, or opportunity outside of God's timing? What happened?
- In what areas of your life do you hear God telling you to be still?

Let us pray:

Dear Lord, I acknowledge that only you have the power to transform me. I believe that you will do it in your own time, which is also the perfect time. Please forgive me for when I have attempted to take matters into my own hands. In order for you to get glory out of my story I know that I have to surrender to you. Your word says that you are a rewarder of those who diligently seek you[1]. So Lord, today I put you first. Fill me with your desires, your patience, and direct my paths. It's in Jesus' name that I pray, Amen.

STAGE THREE

The Pupa

CHAPTER NINE

Hanging on by a Thread

I am the vine; you are the branches. If you remain in me and I in you, you will bear much fruit; apart from me you can do nothing.

—John 15:5, NIV

When the caterpillar has fully grown it sets out to find a safe place from which it will then enter into the metamorphosis phase. Once it finds the branch of its choice, it spins a silk patch that will be used to keep it secure until it is ready to emerge as a new creature, the butterfly[1]. I hope that by now you will have seen changes within yourself, you have deepened your relationship with God, and you are more familiar with His Word. Here is the point where you decide if you're going to stay a caterpillar or if you're going to allow God to have complete control.

I have to be honest with you; the pupa stage was probably one of the loneliest and most exciting stages in my life. I mean it was just me and God. Sure, I was interacting with people on a daily basis, the change that was taking place on the inside of me couldn't be explained to just anyone. I was really starting to separate the old me from the new me, and it was hard. I didn't want to isolate myself, but at the same time I didn't want to be pulled back down to where I had just come. I became very conscious about what I was saying, how I was saying it, and conversations with some people were shorter and less frequent than before. TV shows and music that used to appeal to me all of a sudden didn't appeal to me anymore, and I found myself more intrigued by God than a reality show or the newest song. At times I felt like a cavewoman, but I knew that I needed to disconnect from the world and truly experience God.

The more time I spent with Him, the closer we became. I could actually hear the Holy Spirit speaking to me while studying His Word. As He spoke, I listened and took notes. I wasn't always sure if I had heard Him correctly, and I would simply pray for confirmation. Every time I asked, I would receive confirmation in twenty-four hours or less. Sometimes the confirmation appeared in my morning devotion, others from sermons that were recently preached, and others from social media. I was shocked when someone asked if I had been hiding in the back of their church, which was over 200 miles away, because my messages were along the same lines as their pastor's! That's when I realized that the same Spirit that was in a pastor, was also the same Spirit that was in me. It didn't matter whether or not I had a title. The Holy Spirit speaks to anyone who is bold enough to seek the presence of God. Does that make me a theologian? Not by a long shot. However, I am more excited than ever before to study God's Word with the expectation of receiving revelation.

As I drew closer to God, I also tried to catch glimpses of my future. I would see some things, but I wasn't absolutely sure if the visions I saw were from God or not. I started to move in one direction and wasn't sure if it was the right direction and just kept asking God to show me signs to reassure me. Some days I would be comforted by them and other days I still wasn't sure. Some nights I would pray, write, cry, or just try to sleep off my frustrations of not knowing if God was really with me or what was next. I was literally hanging on by a thread; but I had to decide whether or not I was going to allow God to take me through the rest of the process or give up right where I was.

The first assignment that I was given I failed miserably. I wasn't exactly known as being the friendliest person in my office, and part of my growth was to redeem myself amongst my co-workers. Typically I would come in, speak to the person in the office next to mine, fix my breakfast, and then go about my business for the rest of the day. One particular day I heard the Lord tell me to say good morning to everyone once I got to work. I was thinking to myself, OK, these people are going to think something is wrong with me. I never speak to them when I come in to work, so this was definitely going to be a challenge.

As I was driving to work I was trying to talk myself into it, and I remember telling myself that it would be fine, what they thought didn't matter, that God would reward my obedience, etc. I pulled into the parking lot, got out of the car, was still encouraging myself as I walked to the top of the steps, I turned the door knob, and nothing. I couldn't do it. As much as I wanted to and thought that I could, I just couldn't do it. I spoke to the same woman that I always spoke to, went into my office, and apologized to God. I felt like I had let him down, but I didn't know what else to do. I had missed my opportunity and I had no intentions of psyching myself up for it again the next day. After acknowledging that I had failed, I asked God for another chance. About a month later, I actually went through with it and I've spoken every morning since then. Even though I hated the thought of it initially, after awhile I started to look forward to it. I'm telling you, it may not seem like it at first, but there is so much peace in obedience!

The next assignment I was given was to bless someone in my office with lunch. I thought, great, I have the perfect person in mind. However, I should have known that was a little too easy. The person that I was thinking of was actually off limits because we were friends. I just laughed to myself because I should have known better. But hey, it was worth a try! In reality, the person that I was supposed to bless was actually another manager with whom I had a rocky past. Like most arguments, ours were formulated out of a lack of maturity and miscommunication, and we never really seemed to click. I can't say that I was overly thrilled about it, but I knew that I didn't want to let God down like I had before. I gave the person a card thanking them for their hard work, told them to have lunch on me, and included ten dollars.

My heart was racing the entire time I was preparing the card. I had no idea how it would be received, if they would think I was weird, crazy, or what; but I didn't care. I went through with it, and it actually made their day. Although it took a few hours before they said thank you, I didn't want to focus on that. I knew that I had fulfilled a duty, and I was happy about it. Did we instantly become best friends? No. But there was definitely a dark cloud that was lifted, and I would do it all over again if I had to. It wasn't something that I had to brag about to someone else or expect something in return other than a job well done by God. Your obedience to God has everything to do with your heart, and very little to do with the possible rewards and recognition for your actions. Sometimes you just have to be happy with knowing that you did the right thing, and that God was your only witness.

Some of us have been known to live double lives. We're one way in church and then nobody can tell that we're a Christian anywhere else, including our own homes. I was definitely one of those people. Keep in mind this was going on even while I was reading His Word, studying, praying, leading ministry, etc. on a regular basis. My excuse was always that people in church didn't have time to get on my nerves like other people did so I didn't have a reason to be mean to them. The thing is, when God transforms you there is no selective serving. Everyone is entitled to experience His love, not just church members. I cannot stress enough that this journey will be an ongoing process, and that you are in a pursuit. Don't be discouraged, God will continue to work with you, on you, and in you if you allow Him to.

Up until this point you've been feeding on God's word, growing your faith, and maturing in your spiritual walk. Now it's time to get out of your comfort zone. It's time to take everything that you've been learning and the strength that you've been building, and put it to the test. God may ask you to start doing some things that you would never have thought about doing otherwise. It could be serving others on your job, taking a leadership role in a ministry, serving in the community, etc. Whatever it is, if you're overly thrilled about it, you might want to make sure that God was talking and not you. Trust me, when the assignment comes from God, it usually isn't something that you'll shout about. We typically like doing what makes us comfortable, but that would be too convenient for us. The good thing about it though is that whatever your task, you will have to depend on God to get it done. Ultimately, that's what He wants; for others to see His goodness through you. Besides, you haven't been working hard all of this time just to stay where you are. You've been preparing for something great. You've been preparing for your destiny! So if you don't hang on tightly, you may short-circuit your progress.

Matthew 9:37 says, "Then he said to his disciples, "The harvest is plentiful but the workers are few." I believe that there are many Christians that have made it to this point in their spiritual walks, but then they've let go. I believe their hearts were in the right place, but then circumstances somehow allowed them to be washed away back to where they were. It is also possible that they have just been paralyzed by fear and doubt. They spent so much time in the caterpillar state that their surroundings became comfortable. When the time came for God to move them into the next phase, things got a little scary and fear shook their faith loose. We don't want to lose who we are, but at the same time, we don't realize that who we are is in fact who we were. God has given you a new life that was meant to replace the one that was given to you at birth. It's in you. You just have to set it free.

At this stage you're getting ready for the manifestation of the complete transformation. You've been shedding things that have been weighing you down, revealing this beautiful person that has been in preparation for this moment. When you choose not to transform, the work of the Kingdom is jeopardized. There is a harvest that is out there waiting for you. There are people that God intended for you to reach with your specific gifts, but you've got to hang on. You are so close to where He wants you to be. It may feel like you're all alone, but you're not. God is with you every step of the way, and He's closer than you think. Matthew 19:26 reminds us that with God all things are possible. Not just a few things or specific things, but all things. God is able to take the most unlikely person and use them to bring glory to His name. The only thing standing between you and your destiny is your faith. If you truly believe that God has something better for you, then you can start acting like it right now. You can start positioning yourself for greatness right where you are. You have to trust Him. You have to cling to Him. You have to give Him control. This is not the time to give up and let go, this is the time to completely surrender.

Even though the caterpillar was probably comfortable eating and growing, and eating and growing, it knew there was more. In order to get there, it had to leave where it was and seek an unfamiliar place. It didn't need to take an entourage with it. You have to know when God is moving you and go with the flow. You aren't always going to be able to take everyone with you. You may have to leave some of your friends and family members behind. I know you love them and you have a history, but it's not their destiny, it's yours. You cannot be afraid of being alone. In Matthew 26:40, Jesus was about to be arrested and his disciples were sleeping. You definitely don't need people around you that will go to sleep on you when you need them the most. So embrace this time of connecting with God. He can bring you more friends and allow you to minister to your family at a later time, but right now you have to trust Him.

I remember when I was picking colleges that I wanted to attend, and I knew that I didn't want to stay in Maryland. I had grown up there and I wanted to get out and see new things and meet new people. All of the schools that I chose to visit were in North Carolina. I had a cousin that lived down there, and since we had a close relationship, I trusted that it was a pretty nice place to be. I figured it was far away enough for me to be on my own, but also close enough for me to get home when I wanted to. Sure I had friends in high school, some that I had known for ten years or more, but I had to do what was best for me. Staying in Maryland wasn't it. I had no idea if I would know anyone on campus, but it didn't matter. I just wanted to get away and start a new life. I couldn't worry about who I was leaving behind because we all had our own destinies.

What is keeping you from clinging on to God? What are some of the ties pulling on your heart other than God? Anything that you're not willing to let go of is a tie. Whether it is poor money management keeping you in debt, TV shows or hobbies consuming your evening productivity, bad relationships, etc. What is keeping you from moving forward in your purpose? Jesus says in Luke 9:62, "No one who puts a hand to the plow and looks back is fit for service in the kingdom of God." You can't follow God and stay where you are. You have to choose between going forward or backwards. As much of a chance that I took going to an unknown place, you're going to have to take a chance on God and trust that He's going to be there with you. I can only imagine how vulnerable a caterpillar becomes when it decides to leave the very place it has known since birth to seek a place for transformation. They can literally spend hours trying to find the perfect spot[2]. Somehow, the reward seems so much greater than the risk and they go after it anyway. How badly do you want to be set free to fly in God's purpose for your life?

When we look in Numbers chapter 14, the Israelites were supposed to take a risk. Unfortunately fear stood between them and their reward. Even though the land was occupied by giants, it was the land that God designated especially for them. They just had to be obedient and trust God. Instead, they chose to complain and gave up. That's the difference between pursuing promise and pursuing your purpose. A promise may get your attention, but purpose will keep your attention. See, you can live without a reward if you have to jump through too many hoops to get it or if it inconveniences you. But when you are pursuing a purpose greater than yourself, the mature spirit will say, "Not my will, but thy will be done." Jesus was given a promise of life after death; but in order to get the promise, he had to fulfill his purpose. At one point, Jesus wasn't thinking about the promise because his purpose almost became too much to bear. In Luke 22:42 Jesus says, "Father, if you are willing, take this cup from me; yet not my will, but yours be done." It wasn't the promise that kept him going, it was his purpose. When things get rough, the promise isn't going to keep you submitted to God, but rather your purpose will. So you need to get your spirit ready for this journey.

Unfortunately, the Israelites went after their promise outside of God's timing and perished because He was not with them. They were so focused on the obstacle that stood in between them and their promise that they forgot all about God's purpose. Where God wants to take you, there may be giants occupying the land right now, but He has set aside that place for you. If God made you a promise, then it's yours. However, it is the pursuit of purpose that is going to get your to your promise. Your giant could be a manager, a CEO, a competitor, an illness, opinions of others, lack of resources, guilt, shame, fear, etc. You just have to know and believe in what God has purposed for you and then go after it against all odds. If you commit to the purpose, the promise will come. God wants to get glory out of your story. If you could do it by yourself, there would be no need for Him. So instead of complaining or fearing the obstacle, call out and say "God, this looks like a job for you!" You simply cannot lose if God is with you. Not only is He with you, but He's for you. He's on your side, ready to help you conquer this world. As long as you cling to God, He will continue to cling to you.

If there is something you're holding onto that's keeping you from fulfilling your purpose, you have a very important decision to make. You have to decide if God's purpose is worth more to you than whatever that "thing" is. You will have to completely let go in order to allow God to move you forward. The last shed that the caterpillar makes before revealing the pupa must be released with a violent twitch intended to break the ligament holding the skin[3]. You may have to fight through tears, emotions, and fears, but it's absolutely necessary if you expect to move on. The greater the risk, the greater the reward, and I would be willing to bet on God any day. You can do this. God is on your side. So hang in there, you are so close to being set free.

PREPARING FOR FLIGHT

- Are you struggling between letting go of your comfort zone and moving towards your destiny? What's holding you back?
- Are you chasing after a promise or are you pursuing a purpose?
- When you have felt alone, have you asked God to present himself in order to reassure you that He's still near by?
- What giants are currently occupying the land containing the promises that God has for your life?
- What ties outside of God are pulling on your heart that you need to cut loose today?

Let us pray:

> Lord I thank you for your presence. Even in times when I feel like I am all alone, I thank you for your gentle whispers that reassure me that you are near. Lord, today I want to cling to you. I ask that you sever the ties between me and anything or anyone that is keeping me from fulfilling my purpose. I recognize that my purpose is larger than anything that I could handle on my own, so I put my complete faith and trust in you. I thank you for being patient with me as I continue to draw close to you. It's in Jesus' name that I pray, Amen.

CHAPTER TEN

All Wrapped Up

But he knows where I am going. And when he tests
me, I will come out as pure as gold.

—Job 23:10, NLT

Once the caterpillar secures its grip on the branch of its choice, it completes one final shed to reveal what is called a chrysalis[1]. The caterpillar could be in this state for weeks or for months depending on the season in which it entered. For instance, if the caterpillar pupates in the fall, it may wait until the spring before it emerges. Otherwise the process tends to be quicker during the warmer months. That last shed symbolizes that the caterpillar is preparing to let go and to completely be transformed. There are some things that are easier to let go than others. Maybe some of the bad habits that you needed to break became easier to end as you drew closer to God. You stopped watching certain kinds of shows, you stopped hanging around certain types of people, you changed your attitude at work, etc. Those things become easy after a while, but what is that one last thing that's hanging on to you? Is it bitterness, unwillingness to forgive someone, maybe you owe someone an apology? These are a few deep matters of the heart that will keep you from your destiny.

After being so vengeful for most of my life, I had to learn to forgive. God had to change my heart to be willing to extend the same grace to others that he extended to me, and that was hard. When I wanted to call people out, God reminded me that it wasn't worth it. I would be upset because I felt like I was punking out, and the person needed to know that they couldn't just treat me any ole kind of way. I always felt like people deserved to be repaid for what they had done, but then God would always remind me of His grace, and it would move on my heart. I didn't get it right all of the time, but I was more aware of the conditions of my heart and prayed my way through it. At the very least I wanted to try to be better and I knew that I had to be if I was going to go where God was taking me. I had never prayed for my enemies as much as I did during this time. I realized that the lesson that I wanted to teach them wasn't the message God wanted to portray. What started out as a feeling of weakness, God turned it into humility. It is no coincidence that God is refining you in this part of the process. The word chrysalis is a derivative of the Greek word meaning gold[2]. If you look up a picture of a butterfly cocoon you can actually see gold markings on it.

God is perfecting you for His purpose. So what is that one last thing that's pulling on your heart that you need to let go?

The chrysalis state will feel like you are out in a spiritual wilderness. There isn't anything or anybody that can come between you and God. It can be an uncomfortable feeling, but you have to focus on the purpose of this time. God needs your undivided attention. He is so close to setting you free to fly and He needs to make sure that you're ready to do so. You don't need anyone else in your ear right now except Him. You may get input from all of these external sources and before you know it, something you hear will have you doubting where God is taking you. So cherish this time and really fine tune your ear to God's voice. Get rid of all of the worldly clutter and just enjoy His presence. Throughout the bible we've seen where God has called His children into the wilderness. Their time spent alone with God was for different reasons such as revelation, preparation, restoration, and temptation.

In the third chapter of Exodus, God appears to Moses in the wilderness to reveal to him his call to lead the Israelites out of Egypt. At first God was pretty vague with the instructions that He gave to Moses. He told Moses the overall vision for his plan to lead the Israelites into the land flowing of milk and honey, and then just told him to go. But Moses had a few questions that he needed answered first. Moses questioned his authority, qualifications, and skills for the mission he was to complete. He asked, and God told him where to go, who to talk to, what to say, who to take with him, and what to do. Don't be afraid to talk to God about the visions that He gives you. He may respond with answers as simply as "I will be with you," or "I will provide," but whatever the response, you will need to take that and run with it. And let me reiterate the fact that you should talk TO GOD about the visions that He gives you. After God answered his questions, Moses told his brother Aaron about the plans. He didn't ask him for his opinion on whether or not he should go through with them, if he believed what God said, etc. He told him what they were supposed to do. So make sure you ask God for clarity, and then if you decide to share the vision with someone else, simply make a declaration of what God is going to do in your life. Make sure you share it with someone that you can trust. The last thing you need is someone else trying to tell you how to complete an assignment that God has given you or have them stir up doubt and fear in your heart.

Now, keep in mind that even though Moses was given a great mission to complete, he almost lost his opportunity to complete it. In Exodus 4:24, we see that the Lord appeared to Moses and was about to kill him. The reason being, Moses had a son that was uncircumcised, which meant he was not in a covenant relationship with God based on Old Testament law. If you look in Genesis 17:9-13, God describes the details of the covenant with Abraham that is supposed to be passed down for generations to come. In verse 14 it says, "Any uncircumcised male, who has not been circumcised in the flesh, will be cut off from his people; he has broken my covenant." The circumcision was a sign of being a descendant of Abraham, which also signified being a descendant of God. Since Moses had broken the covenant, he was in jeopardy of being cut off from the very people that he was supposed to set free. The Lord spared Moses only after his wife circumcised their son, thus restoring the covenant.

At this point you may be wondering what circumcision has to do with fulfilling God's purpose for your life. However, it's not about the circumcision in and of itself; it's about the covenant. Just because God gives you a task to fulfill it doesn't negate the need for obedience. While you are no longer subject to Old Testament law, you are still responsible for abiding by the commands of the new covenant set by Jesus Christ. 1 Corinthians 7:19 says, "Circumcision is nothing and uncircumcision is nothing. Keeping God's commands is what counts." By keeping the commands, you in turn honor your covenant with Jesus Christ set forth by your acceptance of salvation. The commandments are simply this, "Love the Lord your God with all your heart and with all your soul and with all your mind. This is the first and greatest commandment. And the second is like it: Love your neighbor as yourself"[3]. While it is exciting to be used by God, we must not forget the responsibility that goes along with it. Although you may be pursuing His purpose, it does not set you above reproach. Just as surely as the Lord gives, He can also take away[4]. As you continue to prepare for your purpose, also continue to guard your heart. You've come too far to have your purpose derailed because of disobedience.

Another person that experienced time in the wilderness before setting out to fulfill his purpose is the Apostle Paul. Paul tells us in Galatians 1:15:17 that when he received his calling from God, he did not consult man or other apostles, but rather he went away to spend time with the Spirit of God. He then later returned to the place that he initially left. Your time in the wilderness isn't permanent. I know you're comfortable with your friends and family, but there is great value in taking a time out from the world and just sitting in the presence of God. The tasks that He has prepared for you are great, and He needs your undivided attention so that He can properly train you for your mission. You may only need to take a one month hiatus from whomever or whatever you're involved. On the other hand it could be a longer period depending on the season and timing of you finally deciding to pursue your purpose. In either case, it won't be forever.

The one thing I've learned is that if you turn your focus away from what you're "losing" and towards what you're gaining, you'll end up with even more in the end. Remember that God loves you and doesn't want to harm you. He just wants to spend time with you the same way you want to spend quality time with someone that you love. Again, as we saw with Moses, he didn't consult someone else about the calling that God gave him. He received his calling and then he went to work. You will need to display that same boldness so that it will boost your credibility. Have you ever encountered someone that was supposed to give you an important message and they could barely get it out right? They can't remember exactly what was said, the person's name, they lost the paper it was written on, etc. Either the sender failed to properly train the messenger or the messenger didn't care enough about the message he/she was supposed to deliver. God doesn't want you going out here and making a fool out of Him. If He's placed a calling on your life, then own it and do what you have to do in order to execute it. He can't make you spend time with Him. You have to know that you need to spend time with Him and then do it. Preparation is key!

We see in Matthew 4 that the Holy Spirit led Jesus into the wilderness in order to test his resistance to temptation. The devil figured that Jesus would be weak after fasting for forty days and forty nights, but Jesus knew better. He was hungry, but he wasn't hungry enough to disobey God. Jesus' mission was riding on his ability to pass the test. He didn't have an audience of men to witness whether or not he was on his best behavior. His audience was God. Fulfilling your purpose is not just for show, it's a lifestyle commitment. You don't get to turn the cameras off and on when you feel like it. God is your audience whether other people are watching what you're doing or not. Just because it seems as if nobody is watching to see if you keep God's commands, noticing that you're smiling more or getting excited during praise and worship, started tithing, etc., your obedience is between you and God. If Jesus succumbed to temptation He may have disqualified himself from being the Savior of the world! God even tested Jesus to make sure that he was fit for service. So you can guarantee that you will be tested too.

The text mentions that Jesus was fasting while he was in the wilderness. Getting close to God may require you to do some form of a fast as well. It could be a fast from certain types of food, social media, TV, music, social outings, etc. In my experience, fasting has not only given me clarity, but it has also helped me build greater discipline and spiritual strength. One year I started off with the Daniel's fast, which includes eating fruits, vegetables, and only drinking water. The next year I attempted fasting from sun up to sun down, eating only before the sun arose and after it set, and drinking throughout the day. Once I accomplished those, I challenged myself with a total fast that lasted for ten days. In the beginning I didn't think I could do it, but each day I continued to pray my way through. There were days that I wanted to quit, but I knew that my obedience and sacrifice would be pleasing to God. The only way I made it through was keeping my focus on Him. The security of knowing that He was there with me pulling me through made all of the difference. The caterpillar actually does not eat during this stage. In fact, it may completely empty any undigested contents from its system before forming the chrysalis[5]. It's taking as little as possible from its old body to the new one.

You may also need to search your own life and determine if there are any additional contents that you're trying to take with you that you shouldn't. Whatever it is, get rid of it now. It will only cause further delays in your pursuit of fulfilling your purpose. Once Jesus passed his test, the angels attended to him, and he was cleared to begin his ministry.

The wilderness can also be used for a time of restoration as depicted in the second chapter of Hosea. In the first thirteen verses we learn about the punishments coming forth to Israel as a result of their disobedience to God. Much like today, they decided to worship man-made idols, forgetting that it was God who had given them everything that they had. However, in the midst of their disobedience God shows how loving He really is. In verse fourteen God says, "Therefore I am now going to allure her; I will lead her into the wilderness and speak tenderly to her." If you continue to read the chapter, God talks about all of the things that He's going to restore to them as if it was the first day He delivered them out of Egypt. God isn't in the condemning business, but rather He's in the restoring business. He sent Jesus to give us a better life, and to free us from condemnation[6]. You can also use this time to restore your relationship with Christ. You've shed the things that weren't like Him, so that now you can start walking in and displaying the fruits of His Spirit. God wants you all to himself and will be gentle with you through this process. He knows whether or not you have a heart to live for Him, and spending time together alone will strengthen your relationship. He wants you to live a great life for Him!

Take this time to really enjoy the presence of God in your solitude. Ask Him the purpose of your wilderness and then let Him work in you. If you're currently pursuing something, don't get discouraged if other people don't help you right away. It may just be God trying to get your attention to give your full trust to Him. It could also be a temporary obstacle. Nonetheless, know that He will provide you with every resource that you need exactly when you need it. This is the time to put your relationship to the test. Can you and God trust each other? Trust is a very important component of your relationship with God. You need to be able to trust Him as much as He needs to be able to trust you. It's not enough to simply celebrate when God has blessed you. Can He celebrate you for being a blessing to Him? The life that you desire is waiting for you, but you have to be willing to let go of what was and continue preparing for what is to come. Allow God to wrap you in his arms, spend some quality time with you, and refine you. You'll be glad that you did!

PREPARING FOR FLIGHT

- Have you ever shut out the rest of the world so that you could spend quality time with God? Why or why not?
- Who or what is keeping you from spending quality time with God?
- What type of fast are you willing to do in order to build up your spiritual strength?
- What is your biggest fear about being in the wilderness?
- What do you hope to learn from God during your time in the wilderness?

Let us pray:

Lord I thank you for wanting to spend time with me to prepare me for my purpose. I desire to hear from you more clearly than ever before. Please give me the courage and strength that I need to cut off external influences. I know that I don't have to fear being alone because you are with me. Lord I ask that you continue to transform and refine me for the sake of your glory. It's in Jesus' name that I pray, Amen.

CHAPTER ELEVEN

The Ultimate Surrender

*Then he said to the crowd, "If any of you wants to be
my follower, you must turn from your selfish ways,
take up your cross daily, and follow me. If you try to
hang on to your life, you will lose it. But if you give
up your life for my sake, you will save it."*

—Luke 9:23-24, NLT

At some point during the pupa stage the caterpillar liquefies
and reorganizes inside of the chrysalis[1]. It essentially loses
its old body for the sake of becoming a butterfly. Even after
spending time with God, listening to his voice, and gaining
clarity on your purpose, you still have a choice. You can either
stay right where you are and keep doing what you're doing
or you can allow God to take you to a whole new level. If you
decide to continue to pursue your purpose, which I hope you do,
know that you are about to open a floodgate of immeasurable

possibilities. But first, you're going to have to be willing to let go of the old you. The old you was more concerned about the things of the world rather than fulfilling your purpose. The old you allowed the opinions of others to keep you from pursuing your destiny. The old you allowed the world to buy you at a discount even after Christ had already paid for your life in full. The new you finds greater delight in spending time with God than sitting idle in front of a TV. The new you is more concerned about being a light unto the world than simply seeking material things. The new you will pursue righteousness on a daily basis rather than relying on grace and mercy as an excuse for living a destructive lifestyle.

You are to carry your new identity with you everyday until the coming of Christ. It isn't something that you can take off and put back on. Once the caterpillar becomes a butterfly it can't go back to the body it once had. Even though you have the choice to live a life in sin, you can commit not to do it. You have come so far, why turn back now? I know you're not perfect, and you won't get it right every day, but it's all about intent. Each day you wake up, you can start it off with saying, "Lord, today I choose to live for you." You can carry that thought with you as you interact with your family, your co-workers, strangers, whomever. At the beginning of every day, you will have to make a conscious effort to let God's light and love shine through you on a consistent basis.

Romans 12:2 says, "Do not conform to the pattern of this world, but be transformed by the renewing of your mind.

Then you will be able to test and approve what God's will is—his good, pleasing and perfect will." Now that the Spirit of God has matured inside of you, you will need to align your mind with your heart. The journey on which you are about to embark is all for the sake of the Kingdom. Change is often difficult, and can be scary, but God is waiting for you. He's waiting to show you off to the world. By showing you off, He's ultimately showing off himself through you. The life that you're leaving behind, He's going to more than make up for it.

I can remember being so scared of the life that God was showing me. Was I going to be ridiculed by people that knew about my past? Was I actually hearing from God? Could I actually be trusted with the task He was giving me? I've seen people that truly have a heart for God, but I've always admired them from afar. I never thought that I was actually anointed or worthy enough to be used by Him. Truthfully, I was more than equipped to do what God was calling me to do, but my mind hadn't caught up with my spirit. The only way to get my mind on the same page was to continue to study God's Word, live out His Word, and declare His plans for my life. Once my mind was aligned, my actions started to follow accordingly. God's way may not make complete sense, you may not be able to see the entire picture, but if you focus on His will He will lead you every step of the way.

Unfortunately for many of us, our own fear and disobedience have delayed the manifestation of God's power here on earth. Instead of complaining about school systems, I can see Christian teachers coming together to create a school system of their own. Instead of complaining about lackluster TV shows, I can see Christians coming together to create a network with shows that are pleasing to God. I don't mean preaching shows, but good family shows that teach lessons, morals, and values. I can see Christian doctors and nurses operating with supernatural healing. I can see Christians coming together to create alternatives to the world's system, but will they have the faith to do it?

Do you know that if you pursue the things of God that you cannot fail? If God is telling you to do it, then do it. I don't believe that God will give you a vision without also providing the means to get it done. God is too faithful to fail you. You have to be willing to pursue Him and His purpose for your life. Pursuing God does not always mean that you are going to stand in a pulpit. A pastor or preacher is simply one function of the entire body of Christ. Every Christian is called into their own personal ministry based on the spiritual gifts that they have been given. Now if you go to God and He tells you that you're supposed to be a preacher, then go do it. At the end of the day, we cannot afford to be afraid to be used by God in any capacity.

I am a person that does just fine from behind the scenes. You can give me an assignment, and I'll take it and run with it from beginning to end, just don't put me in the spotlight. God convicted me with that thought one day, and told me that while I was trying to hide, I was also hiding Him. Then He said to me, you aren't in the spotlight, you are the spotlight. Hearing that gave me a new perspective on pursuing my purpose. Your purpose is to give off light to the world in whatever way that may be. It could be through dance, song, administration, film, food, architecture, finance, you name it. Matthew 5:13-16 talks about being the salt of the earth and the light of the world. You weren't made to be kept in a box. You have a gift that the world needs to see. You have the power to influence generations to come. As well, God is able to function through you outside of a church or religious context. What good is it to simply be a light amongst other lights? He wants to use you to shed light on some of the dark places in the world. I personally love to travel, and pray that my purpose would open up opportunities for me to travel both nationally and internationally for the sake of the Kingdom. You will never know how far God can take you unless you start moving. Remember that God's plans will always take you farther than you could ever take yourself. Are you willing to surrender?

Proverbs 20:24 says, "A person's steps are directed by the Lord. How then can anyone understand their own way?" I struggled for so long trying to get people to like me or love me that I eventually lost who I was. I tried to create my own path instead of trusting God to lead me. I learned the hard way that you can't be who the world wants you to be and be who God called you be. You have to choose. While there were circumstances that I could not have avoided, many of the trials and tribulations that I faced I brought them on myself. I chose to take the scenic route through life only to find myself right back where God intended for me to be. I thank God for his grace and mercy.

God didn't intend for you to go through life struggling in any area. Whether it's your love, money, health, career, etc., you simply have to do it God's way. It may look like everyone else is having fun and living the good life, but at some point they're going to need something more to fill the void that the world is unable to give. When the world's cameras are off, God's camera keeps rolling. He's there to direct and guide you every step of the way, even when you're at your worst. I eventually had to wrap my head around the fact that God's way was better than mine. Isaiah 55:8 says, "For my thoughts are not your thoughts, neither are your ways my ways," declares the Lord." No matter what things looked like, I figured that I needed to yield to Him or else I was going to get in the way like I had done before.

Think about all of the positive influences that you have experienced over the years. I'm talking about people that took a risk and pursued the purpose and passion that God put inside of them. Think about how those people or that person impacted your life. What if that person had been disobedient to their calling? You may not have received from them what you needed at exactly the right time. Many of us are currently out of position. There is somebody that is waiting on whatever gift God has put inside of you. You may not know who, how, when, where, or why, but that does not change the fact that you are supposed to be impacting lives. Pursuing your purpose is not just about taking a risk; there are souls on the line. Jesus wasn't thrilled about having to die on a cross, but through his tears, he still chose to honor the will of God. Thanks to him, we don't have to die in a physical sense. God just needs us to die in a spiritual sense. Psalm 116:15 says, "Precious in the sight of the Lord is the death of his faithful servants." You can cry, scream, fight, and yell, but do what you're called to do. After all, the ways of the world can also make you cry, scream, fight, and yell. So you might as well go through it for the one that loves you rather than for the ones that don't. What a precious sight it will be once you make it through!

Often times we allow pain or the fear of pain to paralyze us. We have to remember that new life is sometimes birthed through pain. Each of our mothers had to go through some pain just to get us here. Jesus had to endure pain in order for us to gain new life. In both cases, the pain didn't last forever, but for a moment. If either of them had aborted their missions just to avoid pain, we would not be where we are today. They had to deny themselves for the sake of someone else. Just as the world population would suffer if women chose not to get pregnant out of fear of labor pains, the Kingdom of God also suffers because God's children do not evolve into who they're called to be. I can only imagine what the caterpillar feels like while its body is transforming. I don't think I would be too comfortable having wings pop up out of nowhere. In any event, the gaining of the wings is greater than the temporary moment of pain.

Your rebirth will be the same way. The pain doesn't necessarily have to be physical pain, but it could be emotional pain. The pain of letting go of what was once comfortable can be hurtful. However, the life that you will gain will make it all worth it in the end. Try not to focus so much on what you are losing, but rather what you are about to gain. God loves you so much that He will give you back what you lost as a result of sacrifice plus more. This is exactly why God needed to build up your spirit in order to prepare you for your purpose. He already knew what you would endure as a result of your obedience. Thankfully, He has also given you exactly what you need to get through it. You just need to surrender to the process. Some would say that it is easier said than done; but what is easier to bear in the long run? Wondering what if or experiencing what is? You could keep on going through life on your terms or you can live the life that has been waiting on you since before you were born. Don't let the fear of being in pain hold you back, and remind yourself that it is only temporary.

I personally have a high tolerance for pain, both physical and emotional. However, I struggled with surrendering to God's grace and forgiveness. Guilt and shame often times still had me wondering whether or not God was really going to use me. I knew that I didn't deserve it, and would not have been surprised if He said no. In the back of my mind I would wonder if God was going to position me so that I could make a fool out of myself to teach me a lesson. That was not the case at all. He showed me how so many people in the Bible had shady pasts but He used them anyway. Moses committed murder, David had a man killed and took his wife, Paul spoke out against God at one point, Peter denied Jesus, and the list goes on. Again, I had to catch my mind up with my spirit, and come to terms with the fact that I had truly been forgiven for everything that I had done. That doesn't mean that you walk around in arrogance, but rather in freedom. More than anything, God's grace is very humbling. I know that God has the power to destroy if He really wants to, but instead He chooses redemption for those that fear and love Him. That is such an awesome feeling to me. I honestly don't believe that you will be able to move forward in your purpose if you are constantly looking over your shoulder. Do not let you or anyone else allow that stuff to keep you captive. Acknowledge it as your past, but then leave it there and move forward. You have given up that life!

Nothing makes my heart smile more than seeing the impact that comes from being in God's will. If I am able to impact one life, the overcoming of all of the doubt, fear, guilt, and pain, makes it worth it. Even you can start there. You don't have to focus on changing a million lives all at once with your gift. If you focus on impacting at least one, the rest will come. You don't have to worry about how, just know that God will. The Bible has already shown us how the suffering of one can impact many for generations to come. God wants to be able to do the same through you, right here, and right now. Will you deny yourself and let Him use you for the sake of the Kingdom? The answer to that question will determine whether or not you will fulfill His purpose for your life and how quickly. You can do this!

PREPARING FOR FLIGHT

- What cross is God asking you to bear?
- Identify the new you. What old things, habits, attitudes, people, etc. will you give up in order to pursue your purpose?
- What negative thoughts are keeping your from aligning your mind with your spirit?
- Do you fully believe that you have received God's grace, forgiveness, and mercy?
- Are you willing to surrender to the call God has on your life?

Let us pray:

Lord, I want to do great things for You. I ask that You would calm any fears or doubts that I may have about fulfilling my purpose. I thank You for Your son Jesus Christ who died so that I might have life. Help me to release the old me so that I might give life to someone else. I know that it is by Your grace that You are still able to use me. Lord, I surrender to your will and your ways. It's in Jesus' name that I pray, Amen.

STAGE FOUR

The Adult

CHAPTER TWELVE

Be Transformed!

If anyone is in Christ, a new creation has come: the
old has gone, the new is here!

—2 Corinthians 5:17, NIV

Look how far you have come! You have accepted Jesus as
Lord and Savior, you have been feeding on God's word to
grow your spirit, you have survived the wilderness, and now
you are here. The old you is gone, and the world is ready for
the unveiling of your transformation. At this point, the now
butterfly releases a hormone that allows it to break free from
the pupa[1]. In a like manner, the Spirit of God will speak to
you and let you know that it is time to move forward in your
purpose. You may not think that you are ready, but you are
fully equipped for this phase of the journey. You do not have
time to sit back and wonder about your abilities, God is with
you and has prepared you according to his standards. In fact,

after the butterfly first escapes from the pupa, if it does not fully extend its wings before they dry and harden, they will become deformed and inhibit the butterfly's ability to fly[2]. I know that you have been used to operating a certain way, but you are not who you used to be. You have changed, and you are more powerful than ever before. It's time to get to know the new you, so you can get ready to fly!

One of the things that really helped me in this phase is that I had to expect to be different. Most of those negative feelings, attitudes, and emotions were put away when I was a caterpillar, growing and shedding. You will have to remind yourself that you have changed on a regular basis until it becomes like second nature. This stuff does not happen overnight. You are still human, and you will continue to be a work in progress until the day that you die. However, you do need to be intentional and consistent about how you present the spirit that is inside of you. Before the behavior is displayed on the outside, you must make the decision to display it in your mind. That was a problem that I had before I was serious about pursuing the things of God. I didn't care whether or not I hurt people's feelings. I wanted to say what was on my mind and whatever the consequences were going to be, and then I would deal with them. I could not wait for people to provoke me, as I like to call it, just so that I could let them have it. I thought it was cute to be mean and hateful, because after all, according to my "sign" I was born to act that way. But the Kingdom of God does not operate under astrological signs. It operates in the image of God. We are supposed to be like Him, and astrology only limits our ability to live in the likeness of Christ as we are called to do. If you were like me, you should expect to find astrology foolish and useless as it pertains to the new you.

There should be certain shows, songs, artists, movies, etc., that do not draw your attention like they used to. A mature spirit does not eat the same things that an immature spirit eats. I keep saying this because it is very easy to get caught up in what is popular even if you are pursuing God. Just because someone suggests something to you, that doesn't mean you have to watch it, listen to it, etc. You have to guard your heart daily. I'm not saying that you can't watch TV, listen to the radio, go to the movies, or whatever else, but I am saying that there are certain things that you should not allow to enter into your spirit. Once those seeds are planted, they will grow over time if you are not careful. 1 Peter 5:8 says, "Be alert and of sober mind. Your enemy the devil prowls around like a roaring lion looking for someone to devour." The devil can use one small window of opportunity to cause you to stumble and fall. Minimize his chances of doing so by keeping your heart as pure as possible. If people think you are weird because you don't engage in all of the same things they engage in, congratulations, you have matured! Meditate on 1 Corinthians 13:11 (NKJV) which says, "When I was a child, I spoke as a child, I understood as a child, I thought as a child; but when I became a man, I put away childish things."

You're not a caterpillar anymore; so don't be surprised if you stand out from people that are still in that phase.

1 Corinthians 2:14 states, "The person without the Spirit does not accept the things that come from the Spirit of God but considers them foolishness, and cannot understand them because they are discerned only through the Spirit." Honestly, you should expect some people to misunderstand you. If the person is not operating under the Spirit of God, they aren't going to understand because it's impossible for them. An immature spirit may not understand the things of a mature spirit. Don't get discouraged. Instead, recognize the difference and move on. If you really want instruction and confirmation on the separation between what is foolish and what is not, read the book of Proverbs. There is enough wisdom in that Book to sustain you for the rest of your days.

As well, there are certain behaviors and emotions that you become more aware of and more intentional about controlling. At one point I could not care less about whether or not somebody thought I was a nice person. I mean I knew that I was nice to people that I wanted to be nice to, and that was all that mattered. But now, I genuinely have a concern for other people and whether or not I am being a light to the world. And there are still a ton of other things that I can improve upon daily, like patience, showing grace and mercy to others, exercising my faith, etc. The simple fact that I am not only aware of my shortcomings, but also committed to minimizing them is a major accomplishment for me. This journey is not just about me anymore as I once believed. Every time I turned someone away because of a negative attitude, I lost an opportunity for them to see God. So I had to work on that, and I still do. You may have other behaviors and emotions that you need to work on, and that's ok. Continue to work on them. You have come too far to allow the things that once held you captive to make you stumble and fall back to where you were.

1 Corinthians 2:15-16 says, "The person with the Spirit makes judgments about all things, but such a person is not subject to merely human judgments, for, "Who has known the mind of the Lord as to instruct him?" But we have the mind of Christ." You have the mind of Christ, so you should expect to approach things with more caution than you did before. The question "What would Jesus do?" is not some fashion statement, but rather it is a way of life. You put away the things of your flesh so that you could exemplify Christ. Now you have to act it out on a daily basis. Make no mistake; just because you have emerged at this stage, it does not mean that you have arrived. There will be days that you fall short, and there will be days that you do not get everything completely right. The key here is to keep your intentions pure and at the front of your mind. You know where you have been, and what it was like to be far from God. As a result, you still have to guard your heart and protect the new life that you have been given. Philippians 4:8 reminds us, "Finally, brothers and sisters, whatever is

true, whatever is noble, whatever is right, whatever is pure, whatever is lovely, whatever is admirable—if anything is excellent or praiseworthy—think about such things." These things are the substance of your wings! Before the butterfly's wings harden, it pumps a yellowish fluid into its wings to help them expand to their full size[3]. You should aim to fill the veins of your wings with whatever is true, noble, right, pure, lovely, admirable, excellent, and praiseworthy so that you can maximize your wingspan. Anything else will simply clog up the flow of the Holy Spirit that is at work in you, and begin to weigh you down and limit your ability to fly. If you are not sure about whether or not something fits into one of those categories, take a step back and ask God for discernment. If it still does not feel right, then it probably isn't.

Understand that you should have something to show for your transformation in every area of your life. Your transformation is not selective, but rather holistic. The butterfly does not pick and choose which body parts it wants to keep from its caterpillar state. It transforms into a completely new creature. The same thing applies to you. While you may not be able to display them all at once, you can certainly work towards them over time. Your finances should look different, your actions should change, your eating habits may change, your attitude should be more positive than before, etc. All of these changes are for none other than the sake of the Kingdom. How will you be able to pursue your purpose if basic stewardship is always an issue? Whatever it may be, get your disobedience out of the way so that you can pursue your destiny.

For some of you, health may be an issue. You should be committed to taking care of your body, not for some public image, but because your body belongs to God. 1 Corinthians 6:19 says, "Do you not know that your bodies are temples of the Holy Spirit, who is in you, whom you have received from God? You are not your own;" The spirit in you cannot do the work of the kingdom if there is no life in the body of which it resides. So take care of yourself. It can be a lot to manage, but that is why you must continue to spend time with God, and keep your mind on him. If you have to wake up everyday and say, "Lord, today I am going to spend less for you," or "Lord, today I am going to eat healthy for you," then do that. I strongly recommend making declarations at the beginning of each day, so that you set the tone right from the start. It is ok that things have changed. You do not have to feel guilty about it, and it does not make you better than anyone else; it just shows how different life is when you focus on the things of God. I eat healthy and exercise regularly, not only for my enjoyment, but also as a responsibility. I stay out of debt because of my commitment to God. If He needs me to do something, I need to be physically, mentally, and financially fit to do whatever it is. Remember, you gave up your selfish desires to pursue the things of Christ. So continue to embrace your transformation and lead by example. Take it one day at a time, and do whatever it is going to take for you to commit to the new life that you are living and fulfill the calling that is on your life.

Not only should you expect to act differently, but continue spending time with God learning about and supporting your new identity. Who does God say that you are? According to Psalm 139:14 you are "fearfully and wonderfully made." God did not make a mistake with you. He had intentions to use you for something great even before you were born. The fact that you may have made mistakes in the past does not change who you are in God's eyes. Every intricate detail about you is exactly where it needs to be. Do you believe that? The rest of verse 14 says, "Your works are wonderful, I know that full well." You have to know with full confidence that you are a wonderful work of God. And you are, because His word says that you are. Your new identity is not based on your past or the opinions of others, but it is based on who God says that you are. He has been leading and guiding you throughout this entire transformation process, and knows exactly what He is working with.

For a while I had a hard time letting go of my old image and reconnecting with the image God had of me. God helped me realize how beautiful I was, not some external source. A few people would ask if I modeled and would say that I was pretty, but none of that mattered because I did not believe it myself. Some people would get offended and accuse me of not being able to take a compliment, without realizing that it had very little to do with them, and everything to do with me. Beauty takes form from the inside out, not the other way around. I just thank God that he is able to undo the damage that was done while I was being made fun of when I was younger. So now, embracing the spirit of beauty is something that I try to do for God because he is the one that made me and blessed me with it. I want to be the best person that I can be for Him. I stopped trying to find approval from man, and turned to the Bible for my identity instead.

One of the scriptures that really helped me, and still helps me, is 1 Samuel 16:7. I'm glad that God looks at the heart, while the world tends to look at outward appearances. Sometimes we are harder on ourselves than God is. Any time I would start to get down, I would remind myself that God could see what was in my heart. He knows that I have a desire to change and to pursue him, even in the midst of some of my mistakes. He knows my struggles and insecurities, and helps me work through them. He loves me and He loves you too. God looks beyond your past and your present, and into your future. He wants to help you get to where you are going. In order to do that, you have to learn to see yourself as God sees you. You can't focus on your destiny and your deficiencies simultaneously. One moves you forward while the other holds you back. God needs you to be confident with your identity so that you can inspire someone else to be confident with theirs. That does not mean that you should be arrogant. However, you should acknowledge that you are the perfect imperfection selected to be used by God. It is through grace and love, not your qualifications, that you have been destined to fly. So spend time with God and let him show you who you really are.

While you are exploring your identity, also explore the powers that you have through Christ. John 14:12 says, "Very truly I tell you, whoever believes in me will do the works I have been doing, and they will do even greater things than these, because I am going to the Father." You have the power to do the same works that Jesus did, and more. You have the power to lead others to Christ so that they might experience the goodness of God. I'm not saying that you are going to be able to go around turning water into wine or anything, but I am saying that God will give you the ability to lead others to Christ in your own way. You will have to go to God and find out how He wants to do those works through you. Know that you have the power to change lives. That is what fulfilling your purpose is all about. If what you are doing has not drawn someone else to Christ, you may need to reevaluate either what you are doing or how you are doing it. Like I said before, just because you have emerged, it does not mean that you have arrived. It is imperative that you continue to spend time with God, study His Word, and let Him guide you along this journey. You have come a long way, but you are just getting started in this next phase. Not to mention, you still have to eat!

Along with making sure its wings are fully spread, the butterfly also has to fuse its tongue together so that it can function properly or else it will starve and die[4]. Proverbs 18:21

says, "The tongue has the power of life and death, and those who love it will eat its fruit." As you mature, your tongue ought to mature as well. You should have a taste for God's sweet Word rather than the world's toxins. The world can tell what you've been eating by what comes out of your mouth. There is power in your words, so use them wisely throughout your daily interactions with others, and also spend time in prayer. Prayer is also another powerful tool, whether it is for you or for someone else. The more time you spend with God and study his word, the better your prayer life will become. You will only be able to put out what has already gone in. Continue to feed on God's word and fuse your tongue to it so that you may continue to give life to the new you.

I know that all of this may seem like a lot, but it really isn't. It is just something new. The fact that you have not arrived should keep you motivated to continue your walk with God. Do not be discouraged or attempt to embrace all of your changes in one day. It is still an ongoing process to which you will have to commit. Over time, things will become second-nature to you, just as they did when you were more focused on the world. The good thing is you get to start over. God has given you another chance to experience the life that He destined for you to have from the beginning. Have fun and enjoy the person that you have become!

PREPARING FOR FLIGHT

- How does it feel to become the person that God has called you to be?
- Who do you want to see grow in their relationship with Christ?
- What are some of the biggest challenges that you have overcome thus far?
- What are some of the areas that still need developing?
- Who does God say that you are?
- How are you going to continue to support the new life that you have been given?

Let us pray:

> Lord, I thank you for second chances. I thank you for making this new life available to me even in the midst of my mistakes. Help me to continue to draw close to you. I know that I still have work to do, so please continue to grow and develop me. I believe that you have given me the power to change lives, and I ask that you lead me in the right direction. I thank you in advance for those that will come to know you through my works. It's in Jesus' name that I pray. Amen

CHAPTER THIRTEEN

Flight Preparation

For which of you, intending to build a tower, does not sit down first and count the cost, whether he has enough to finish it—

—Luke 14:28, NKJV

At this point, if you have some idea of what God's plans are for your life, you are actually going to have to sit down and start planning out your course. While it is great to know what God wants you to do, you also need to figure out what you are going to need to execute it. If God is telling you to start a business, then you need to put together a business plan, and do research on all of the paperwork, filing requirements, fees, etc. that you will need to establish the business. If God is telling you to write a book, then you need to start researching publishing options, costs, manuscript formatting etc. Whatever it is, you have to show God that you are actually sold on his vision and then start positioning yourself to walk in it. James 2:17 AMP says, "So also faith, if it does not have works (deeds and actions of obedience to back it up), by itself is destitute of power (inoperative, dead)." God did not give you a vision or task just so that you could dream about it coming to pass. He gave it to you so that you would get to work and get it done. You may not have a clue right now as to how God is going to work it out, but I guarantee you that once you start moving, He will lay out all of the resources that you need to get it done.

When I first sat down to start writing this book, my entire approach had changed from when I had tried to write books in the past. Before, I would sit down and write whenever I would feel like it; I didn't have a true outline, and had not done research on book publishing or anything. This time around, because I felt like it was something that God asked me to do, things were different. I told God that if this is what he wanted me to do then we were going to have to do it together. The first thing I did was set up a writing schedule. I am someone that absolutely loves and needs to work on a deadline. Otherwise, whatever it is, it is not going to get done in a timely manner. I was intentional about getting this done. No TV during the week, except one or two shows on occasion, but that was it. I still work full-time, so I knew I was going to have to make a few sacrifices in order to get this done. The next thing I was did was start researching publishers and manuscript requirements. I had no idea before that there were formatting rules, I was just typing away. I found that some publishers can only be approached by agents and not individual authors, and the fees for publishing varied across the board. There were also things to consider such as the book size, the number of pages, cover designer, etc., and I just kept getting ready so that God could make His move. Once I gathered most of the basic information, I still wanted to make sure that I understood the process and that I established a realistic budget for the project.

I stayed in prayer asking God to lead me to the resources that would allow me to make this a great project for Him, and He did. At one point he led me to a self-publishing webinar that was not only cost-efficient, but full of great information that I needed. So I was encouraged because I felt like God had heard me, He was with me, and that my labor was not in vain. God wants to be with you every step of the way as well. I have often heard people speak of things that they want to change, but then they do not come up with a plan to execute the change. You can beg and plead with God for a promotion, a house, a better relationship, a new business venture, ministry, etc, but then you have to be willing and ready to put in the work. Faith is not magic, and God is not a genie. As aforementioned, James 2:17 AMP says, "So also faith, if it does not have works (deeds and actions of obedience to back it up), by itself is destitute of power (inoperative, dead)." Faith and works is a package deal. You cannot have one without the other and expect to fulfill the calling that

God has on your life. Either your labor will be in vain, or your faith will be useless. The two together, however, work in tandem to attain God's glory. What dreams have been dying inside of you because of your lack of faith? How many opportunities have you let pass you by? Who are you leaving uninspired and unchanged due to your lack of works? There is somebody counting on you to do the thing that God has called you to do! If you would just put the ball in motion, God will make sure that it keeps rolling.

Some of my favorite and most encouraging stories in the Bible are the ones where it appears as if what the characters have is not enough, but then once God comes on the scene, and they follow his instructions, they end up with more than enough. In 2 Kings 4:1-7, we learn about a widow whose sons were about to be taken in as slaves because she had outstanding debts and no way to pay them. When the prophet Elisha asked her what she had, she said that she had nothing except a jar of oil. The little bit that she had was more than enough. Elisha tells her to go collect as many empty jars as she can from her neighbors, and once she did so, he was able to multiply the oil that she had to fill all of her jars. Not only did she have enough to pay off her debts, but she had enough left over to live on. At the beginning, she said she had nothing "except" a jar of oil. So many of us minimize what we have, and allow it to keep us from going after our destinies. I don't have anything "except" a few dollars. I don't know anyone "except" a few people. I don't have any extra time, "except." I don't have anything to wear, "except." We start to make excuses and minimize what we have instead of acknowledging God's ability to maximize everything that He has given us. If you would just start pouring out what you have in you, God will multiply the resources that you need to continue fulfilling your purpose. You may not have any idea how or why things just keep flowing through you, but just as long as you keep looking for people to pour into, God will make sure that you have something to pour. You just have to come up with a plan to start with the little that you have and leave the rest to God.

Another passage that encourages me is Luke 5:1-8. Jesus gets into Simon's boat, tells him to go out beyond the shore into the deep waters, and let down his nets. The first thing Simon does is talk about how unsuccessful he and the other fishermen have been at catching fish. Sometimes we do that as well. We let our past failures keep us from taking a risk on something new. You may have tried to start a business in the past, but since that one did not work out, you hesitate to start another one. You may have had bad relationships in the past, so you will avoid any new opportunities to keep from getting hurt. Your job did not offer you that raise or promotion the last time you asked so rather than risk rejection, you hesitate to ask again. Perhaps those other times, you were trying to move on your own terms instead of on God's. It is not that God does not desire for you to have things and success, but he does not want those things to have you. He will wait to release some things to you until you are ready, and to remind you who is in control. Even though Simon had not caught any fish, he throws out his nets anyway because Jesus told him to. Once he did as he was told, he caught so many fish that the nets started to break, and he needed the other fishermen to help him bring them back to the shore.

What I love about this passage is that we see how Simon's obedience then led to his abundance, not the other way around. When you focus on the obedience of God, abundance will come. God is waiting on you to let down your net so that he can draw others to the gifts that He has placed inside of you. But if you only focus on how much money you are going to make or how many people are going to notice, you will miss it. Whatever God is calling you to do, there may not be a lot of money or people involved at first, and you have to stay committed enough to keep going. If you focus on your obedience to God, the rest will follow. The other thing that these verses showed me is that you have to be willing to allow God to take you out into the deep waters in order to get the catch that He has prepared for you. He did not call you to stay on the shore with everyone else. He wants to separate you from the crowd and use you for His glory. Simon caught so much fish that he needed help hauling it in the boat. How many people will you lead to Christ as a result of your obedience to God? Will you lead so many people that you need others to help you carry the load?

Even in these two small examples, we see the power of faith and works, working together to showcase God's power.

What vessels are you supposed to be pouring into? What nets are you supposed to be casting out? I have heard so many people say that they are "waiting on God," but the truth is God is waiting on us. He has already mapped out your destiny, and you just have to walk the course. Standing still is not going to get you very far. I am not talking about the kind of stillness that you may need in order to get clarity from God, although I do believe that we need those moments from time to time. However, I am talking about just sitting around and waiting hoping that you will stumble upon whatever is supposed to happen next. God did not intend for you to just stumble upon anything. He intended for you to pursue your purpose with boldness and assurance. After all, you have been given a purpose for a specific reason, so of course He wants to make sure that you complete your assignment. He just needs a commitment from you to do whatever it will take to get the job done. If you really believe that God has placed a specific calling on your life, then your works will back up what you supposedly believe. Don't you want to show off who God is and what He is able to do? After all that He has done for me, I am just glad to have a part to play in this thing called life, let alone share a stage with Him.

The Apostle Paul says in 2 Corinthians 12:10, "That is why, for Christ's sake, I delight in weaknesses, in insults, in hardships, in persecutions, in difficulties. For when I am weak, then I am strong." Paul knew that he was not alone in his walk. He didn't mind being presented with opportunities where he would be able to brag about the power of God. But see, we have to be willing to put God in a position to show himself through us. It goes beyond God showing up in the nick of time to keep your lights on. If you were managing your money according to His rules in the first place, you may not have been in that situation. However, God's power is made perfect in weakness. That means you have to be willing to look like the underdog. Notice I said "look like." Because to the world, they may not be able to comprehend how or why you were able to do what God called you to do. But, you will have known all along that by positioning yourself, and getting ready, God would show up and make himself known in the presence of all of your doubters. If it seems a little scary, great. If you think you are going to be vulnerable, you're right. Is there a chance that you may be wrong? Yes. All of these things are possibilities, but they are of little significance. They are only as big as you make them. Someone once told me that you miss 100 percent of the shots that you never take. Just because you have the possibility of missing, do not let that stop you from taking the shot. Eventually, one will go in, and it will be the biggest shot of your life.

If we truly believe God's word in Philippians 4:13 NKJV, "I can do all things through Christ who strengthens me," then our actions will show it. That does not mean doing only the things that you like to do, or the things that are easy and comfortable, or when it is convenient for you. That means relying on the power of God to pull you through the seemingly impossible tasks that He is calling you to do. So often we like to use that verse to hype ourselves up when there is something that we really want to do, but when God asks us to do something, all of sudden that verse doesn't seem fitting. God may be telling you to forgive someone that you think is unforgivable; that is categorized under "all things." God may be telling you to give of your time and money for something specific; that too is classified under "all things."

While you are making plans in the natural, make sure that you are preparing spiritually as well. Ask God to reveal, prepare, and settle the matters of your heart. You may be walking in God's will, but that does not make you invincible from negative attacks. In fact, you are walking around with a big target on your back. But when you know the end of the story, before it begins, you don't have to worry about the struggles and the battles. Jesus revealed the outcome in John 16:33 when he said, "I have told you these things, so that in me you may have peace. In this world you will have trouble. But take heart! I have overcome the world." Not only should you expect trouble to come, but you should expect to overcome your troubles. If that is not the greatest spoiler alert, then I do not know what is! So make your plans, get ready for battle, and go out and rock this world!

Whatever God has called you do, start making your plans now. Do your research, start saving, set a timeline, establish goals, etc. Don't focus so much on what you don't have, but focus on how you can get started with what you do have. I guarantee you that once you start to put your faith to work God will start to put his power to work. Your obedience will set off a domino effect in the Kingdom. The tasks that seemed nearly impossible before you started will began to pick up momentum right before your very eyes. God is on your side and is waiting to do great things through you. Show Him that you are ready to go after your calling!

PREPARING FOR FLIGHT

- Do you currently have a plan to fulfill your calling?
- What resources do you have available to you right now to get started?
- Have you researched the additional resources that you will need?
- In what ways can you put your faith to work to show God that you are preparing for your assignment?
- Who will benefit most from your obedience to your calling?

Let us pray:

> Lord, I pray that you would give me the courage to start with what I have. I know that it may not be a lot, but it is more than enough for You. I ask that You will continue to guide my footsteps and lead me to the resources and people that I need to complete my assignment. Today, I declare that I will put my faith to work. I thank you in advance for everyone that will be blessed because of my obedience. It's in Jesus' name that I pray, Amen.

CHAPTER FOURTEEN

Just Fly

Our deepest fear is not that we are inadequate.
Our deepest fear is that we are powerful beyond
measure. It is our light, not our darkness, that
most frightens us. We ask ourselves, who am I to
be brilliant, gorgeous, talented, fabulous? Actually,
who are you not *to be? You are a child of God.*

—Marianne Williamson,
A Return to Love: Reflections on
the Principles of "A Course in Miracles"

You have come all of this way, and now it's time for you to leave the branch on which you have emerged. It is time to get out of your comfort zone once again, and let the world see what a wonder you are. There is a powerful work going on inside of you that the world needs to see. You don't have a lot of time, so get going! The butterfly does not have a long lifespan, so its primary focus is on mating and creating new life[1]. Your goal is to lead others to Christ by way of fulfilling your purpose. Romans 13:11 says, "And do this, understanding the present time: The hour has already come for you to wake up from your slumber, because our salvation is nearer now than when we first believed." James 4:14 says, "Why, you do not even know what will happen tomorrow. What is your life? You are a mist that appears for a little while and then vanishes." You are already behind schedule, so you need to have a sense of urgency at this point. I can tell you that once you get moving, God will accelerate your progress so fast that you will have to try to keep up with Him. He has been waiting on you, and is so excited to set you free to complete your tasks. So get ready to fly!

Before I started to fly in my purpose I was constricted by something called comparison. I knew that God wanted me to be a speaker, but the first thing I did was begin to compare myself to other speakers. And the thought of it tortured me because I knew that I was not an outgoing person. Most of the speakers that I saw were so animated, open, and loud, and that was not my personality. When I started my blog on finances I focused on the fact that I was neither a financial advisor nor that knowledgeable about the Bible. There were blogs with millions of views and I barely had a thousand. In the midst of my frustration and discouragement, God spoke to me. He made me realize that He was not worried about what I did not have, because by His power, He was going to highlight what I did have. I may not have had the same personality as someone else, but I had my own personality. I may not have had the same volume or tone in my voice as someone else, but I had my own voice. I may not have been certified in finance or theology, but God is able to give me wisdom. You may not think you have it all, but you have just enough for God to get glory out of you. If you would just put what you do have to work, God will make up the difference. You will find that your deficiencies will enhance your dependency on God, and that is exactly what He wants. So rejoice and be glad that you do not have to fulfill your purpose on your own. Embrace God's assistance and go do what He has called you to do!

In Matthew 25:14-28 KJV, we learn about the parable of the talents, or bags of gold as worded in other translations. The man that was given five talents doubled what he had, the man that was given two doubled what he had, and the man that was given one buried it in the dirt. The two men that doubled their talents were given the opportunity to manage even more, while the one that hid his talent ended up losing everything that he had. Even though he had less than the other two, he could have at least doubled what he had and he would have been given the opportunity to manage even more. But because he did nothing, he lost both his talent and the opportunity. My question to you is what treasure has God given you that you have buried in your heart? We want God to give us more, but He wants us to work with what we have.

I had no idea that joining a public speaking club would have led me to teach a Financial Peace class, speak at a women's conference, start a blog, or write a book. None of that happened because I was qualified. All of that came after I took the first steps of faith and obedience. If God had shown me all of that at the beginning, I probably would not have believed it or would have been too afraid to do anything about it. Just like I did not believe that I was hearing from Him years ago when he showed me exactly what I would be doing to fulfill my calling, which was helping others discover their purpose. Likewise, God is not going to reveal to you every single detail of your future. In fact, it may scare you from taking the first step. The tragedy is, if you do not take the first step, you close off the future opportunities that He has waiting for you. Start with the one thing that you have, and trust that God will make you ruler over something bigger in the future.

Time, money, and fear cannot be used as excuses forever. You have the same twenty-four hours to use every day. Your minutes do not carry over and you cannot buy any extra ones when your time runs out. So how can you make the most out of the time that you do have? At one point, I would say I was too tired to pursue my purpose after working all day. I just wanted to come home and relax after all the junk that I put up with during the day, and I thought I deserved it. While that may have been true, relaxing was not getting me any closer to my destiny. I could complain about how tired I was and how I "needed" to watch my favorite shows, but that was not going to change anything.

Your purpose is not going to fall in your lap and wait for you to pick it up. You have to go after it. You have to make time in your schedule every day to push you closer to your goal. Whether it is reading, writing, networking, studying, praying, or researching, do whatever you have to do to make progress. Nobody else can fulfill your destiny except for you. It is either going to get done or it isn't. That is the decision that you have to make and live with. Even if you feel like you are too old or you have missed your prime, there is still something that God can do through you. He is not worried about your age; he is more concerned about His Kingdom. He will use whoever is willing to be used to get the job done. If money is an issue, figure out how you can better manage what you have. God is not going to drop a million dollars in your lap when you can barely save any of what you have already been given. We go back to the issue of the talents again. Well God, I don't have a million dollars or I'm not out of debt, so I'm not going to do anything. That is not the attitude to have. You have to go to God and say, "God, this is what I have, show me how to make the most of it."

The other thing that is helpful is learning how to bargain with people. My philosophy is that everything is negotiable. The worst thing that could happen is that the person tells you no. On the other hand, the best thing that could happen is that you get a great deal and experience God's favor. Really try to make an effort, and watch God make moves on your behalf. The fear factor, well we know that fear does not come from God anyway. 2 Timothy 1:7 NKJV reads, "For God has not given us a spirit of fear, but of power and of love and of a sound mind." If you are experiencing fear, you need to pray that out of your spirit so that you can move forward into your calling.

I know what it feels like to be uncertain, insecure, and whatever else. But that is what this faith walk is all about; believing before receiving. When I finally started to pursue my purpose God was there every step of the way. He had been there for me before, but I knew that He was now in the driver's seat. If I was not sure that I was hearing from Him, I would ask him to speak, and just sit still and wait to hear from him. Sometimes He would speak through e-mail devotionals that I received, sermons, or just directly to me throughout the day. Hearing from Him would give me the burst of energy that I needed to keep going. Once I took one step, it was like He would show me about five more that I was supposed to take. I would say, "Wait a minute God, you are moving a little too fast." He would reply to me and say, "No, you need to keep up!" I would just laugh to myself and quickly oblige reminding myself that He had everything under control. God understands how you feel. Don't be afraid to turn to Him with your issues and feelings. Your purpose is a journey between the two of you, and He will give you the answers and courage that you need.

If you look in Judges 6, you will read about a young man name Gideon who God also called for a great task. He was to deliver Israel from the Midianites with just an army of three hundred men. When the angel of the Lord tells Gideon of his task, he makes excuses that his clan is the weakest and that he is the least in his family. Once again, the Lord reassures him that He will be with him. I hope that by now you are starting to see a pattern in the types of people that God has chosen for great callings. The people that He chose were not perfect and did not fit the typical superhero descriptions. Why is that? It is because God wanted to get the glory out of their story. Gideon had well over thirty thousand men in his army, but God reduced it to three hundred so that others would know that it was Him who helped them complete their task. God wants to do the same thing with you. People should wonder how in the world you are doing what you are doing. You may not be the smartest, the prettiest, the strongest, the most popular, the richest, or have the most prestigious degrees, etc, but you have the power of God working inside of you.

Romans 8:30-31 says, "And those he predestined, he also called; those he called, he also justified; those he justified, he also glorified. What, then, shall we say in response to these things? If God is for us, who can be against us?" The destiny that God has spoken over your life cannot be stopped by anyone else. That does not mean that you won't face any obstacles, but that does mean that your obstacles don't stand a chance against you and your God! So if God says that he is with you, then go. The time that you should be worried is when God is not with you. In that case, you need to be still and wait until you receive further instruction. Otherwise, continue to press on towards your purpose.

Even now, you still may be wondering how you will know if you are hearing from God. I completely understand how you feel. The one thing that I have learned is that you have to be bold enough to ask God to confirm what you have heard or seen. Sometimes you may have to go to God and say, "Lord, give me a sign that I'm on the right track." Gideon asked for confirmation from God in Judges 6:36-40. The first time he placed a piece of wool on the floor and asked God to wet the fleece, but keep the ground around it dry, and God did it. For some reason, that was not enough proof, so Gideon then asked God to wet the ground but to keep the fleece dry, and God did it. I myself have asked God for confirmation on certain things and he has given it to me. That does not necessarily mean that I have a lack of faith, but sometimes I just need confirmation that God is still with me. It is no different than you and another person walking through a house in the dark. You may hear their footsteps for a while, but then once you realize that you don't hear or sense them near you anymore, you would call out to them to confirm that they are still with you. Unless that person is mean or playing a joke on you, they will respond pretty quickly in order to calm your fears. If they do not respond, you would not just keep walking. You would stop where you are, and continue to call out until you could identify some type of response. You can take that same approach with God. Psalm 48:14 reminds us, "For this God is our God for ever and ever; he will be our guide even to the end." He loves you and will give you what you need to keep you moving in the right direction. He wants to be there with you, leading and guiding you for the rest of the days to come. If you will just take that first step of faith, God will encourage you to take many more.

Whatever it is that God is calling you to do, start with the number one in mind. Focus on the one step that you need to take, the one person's life you will affect, the one change that you can make, the one hour that you can spare, etc. Don't lose sight of the bigger picture, but break it down into smaller, manageable steps so that you can keep making progress. Every seed that you sow into your destiny has value. Galatians 6:9 KJV tells us, "And let us not be weary in well doing: for in due season we shall reap, if we faint not." You may not see the harvest right away, but keep planting and keep working, and soon you will see the fruit of your labor. Be confident with the task that God has given you. You don't need to compete with anyone else because the job that you have been given has your name on it, and always has. You don't have to work to qualify for it because God has already chosen you. You have your wings, now it is time for you to fly. So get going, your destiny awaits you!

PREPARING FOR FLIGHT

- What comparisons have you been making that are keeping you from flying in your purpose?
- Identify the insecurities, fears, and excuses that have been holding you back.
- If God could give you more of something, what would you want that one thing be?
- How can you make the most out of what you currently have? For example, time, talent, and money.
- What do you need God to do to confirm that his presence is with you?

Let us pray:

> Lord, I come to you asking for courage and wisdom. I acknowledge that You have destined me to do great things, and that you have equipped me perfectly. Please help me to lay aside all fears, comparisons, doubts, and insecurities. I believe that You are with me, and that you will never leave nor forsake me. Set me free to fly. It's in Jesus' name that I pray, Amen.

CHAPTER FIFTEEN

Don't Lose Sight of the Ground

"Therefore go and make disciples of all nations, baptizing them in the name of the Father and of the Son and of the Holy Spirit, and teaching them to obey everything I have commanded you. And surely I am with you always, to the very end of the age."
—Matthew 28:19-20, NIV

Often times it is so easy to get caught up in what we are doing that we forget why we are doing it. The pursuit of your purpose is not just about what God can do for you, but also what God wants to do through you. Jesus did not come just so that we could secure our place in heaven, pray for everyone else, and hope that they make the decision to accept him. Jesus did not say, sit around and pray that people will follow him. He told us to go and make disciples. That means that you have to actually interact with people with the intention of getting them saved and inspiring them to follow Christ just as you are. Your purpose is to continue the circle of life that once began in you. It is great that you have wings and that you are able to fly, but in order to start new life, you may have to go back down to where you came. The adults do not just fly around basking in the fact that they are no longer limited to a life on the ground, they know that they have work to do and only a short time frame to get it done. The butterfly only lives for one or two weeks after it matures, which creates the urgency for reproduction[1]. After the adult butterflies mate, and the female becomes pregnant, she must then search for host plants on which to lay her eggs[2]. She does not just drop them from the sky and hope that they safely land on the right plant. Instead, she is intentional about the task and responsibility that she has been given. Does that mean that you have to get pregnant in order to go make disciples? No. The point is, God has impregnated all of us with a gift that was meant to be deposited back into the world in order to continue the work of Christ.

Not only do you need to spark new life, but you also need to encourage others that are still growing. In order to inspire a caterpillar, you have to go back to the ground and let them see how God has transformed you, and encourage them to let Him do the same for them. After all, at some point or another in your life I am sure that a butterfly once inspired you to become more than you were. So why not bless someone else? I know that some states have a learning initiative that is called "No Child Left Behind," but the church's mission is that there is No Sinner Left Behind. There is no greater mission on the earth than that. It does not matter how much money you make, how famous you are, how many awards you win, or any of that. Kingdom success is measured by the number of people that are reconciled to God. Proverbs 3:6 NKJV says, "In all your ways acknowledge Him, and He shall direct your paths." God's glory has to be at the center of your pursuit of all things. Your relationships can draw others to Christ, your work ethic, your physical appearance, your discipline, your generosity, etc. God can use any area of your life to draw someone to Christ. Keep that in mind as you go about your daily routines.

On your mission to draw others to Christ, expect to see a crowd. If you do not have any followers, then you should probably assess how you are leading your own life. There will be people that want to support you, people that may want to see you fail, and people that just want to watch and see what you will do next. Then there will be those that want to be as sold out for Christ as you are based on how they see God moving in and leading your life. Think about all of the different people that made up the crowds that followed Jesus and why they were following him. It was because of His works that he drew supporters, haters, and spectators. The works that God has assigned to you should have the same effect. So as your following grows, remain humble. After all, they should not be fans of yours personally, but rather they should be in awe of the spirit that is in you. Whomever you decide to keep closest to you, they should not only help bring out the best in you and keep you grounded, but make sure that at some point they discover their own calling as well.

The point is not for you to just showboat around so that people can look at you. The goal is to be a witness for others. In Matthew 9:9-12, we see that the Pharisees are taken aback by the fact that Jesus is associating with tax collectors and sinners. Seriously, why would the Son of God hang around people that are seemingly less than worthy of his presence? But we can all attest to the fact that none of us is worthy enough to be associated with Jesus, but God loves us that much. After the "haters" question the company that Jesus is keeping, Jesus replies to them in verse 12 saying, "It is not the healthy who need a doctor, but the sick." Can you imagine what the world would be like if no matter how far we climbed the ladder of success, that we never lost sight of the ground? Jesus is saying he doesn't need to hang out with holy people; those aren't the people that need him the most. Instead, he associated himself with people that needed a change of heart and a good role model to follow. Keep that in mind as you pursue your calling. God isn't raising you up just so that you can sit around and look down on people that are still where you once were. He's raising you up so that you can spark a desire to know Christ in someone else. You can't do that if you are only hanging around other butterflies all of the time.

At least if you are, then go minister to someone else together as a group. Even though you are flying in your purpose, you still have a job to do that involves others. While the world may be in a rat race to see who can make the most money, God's children should be racing to see who can make the most disciples before the return of Christ. One of the best ways to do that is through service.

When we think about Jesus, and the crowds that followed him, they followed him because he had something that they needed. Whether it was healing, forgiveness, life, rescuing, food, etc, He had gifts that he was openly willing to share with others to prove that he was the Son of God. Even with all of the power that He had, he acknowledged the one that gave him the power, and remained humble. We see in John 13:5 that Jesus washed the disciples' feet. Can you imagine the CEO of a major corporation washing the feet of a janitor? Maybe not even washing their feet, but what about treating them to a nice lunch or dinner. Talk about humility. When you get down to John 13:14 Jesus says, "Very truly I tell you, no servant is greater than his master, nor is a messenger greater than the one who sent him." Understand that you are now a servant and a messenger of the Kingdom. You are no longer the focal point, but rather the spirit that lives in you. Anytime you deny yourself, you allow God's light to shine through you. Ultimately, your purpose is to serve this world with the gifts that God has given you. He gets all of the credit for how great you are, and you should be willing to share him openly with others. How can you be a blessing in this day and age to prove that you are not only a believer, but a follower of Christ? Will it be through your generosity, your love, your spirit of excellence, etc? Who can you serve to give them hope that God still exists, even in the midst of all of the chaos that we see today?

I can honestly say that I have found such an inner peace by just letting go and letting God take control. I am thankful that He has not held my past against me, and I have never been more excited to pour into someone else the love that He has poured into me. I do not think that I would feel the way that I do if it were not for the trusting relationship that I have developed with Him. I no longer fear not being loved, being good enough, or being pretty enough. I trust the plans that He has for my life, and I choose to play by his rules. If someone had asked me years ago "why should I believe in your God?" I honestly don't know what I would have said. Probably something short of to save your soul from going to hell. While that is true, I have found that there is so much more. Believing in my God keeps me alive. He makes life more meaningful and worth living, right here, and right now. He is my biggest supporter, and my number one fan. He loves me more than I could ever know, and I owe him my life. He has proven himself to me time and time again, and for that I will be forever grateful.

You see, salvation is about more than just reconciling our souls back to God. Salvation is just a starting point to becoming all that God has called us to be. You are not supposed to get saved and then stay the same. There is so much more in store for you than wearing a cross around your neck, going to church, or reciting the Lord's Prayer. Salvation opens the door to new life, but you have to walk through it. God has shown me that he gave us the gift of the Holy Spirit for restoration, transformation and continuation. I was restored to God the day that I accepted Jesus as Lord and Savior. However, I was not transformed by the Holy Spirit until years later when I surrendered to God's will. My transformation did not come from practicing religion or following strict rules. My transformation came from the revelation of who God is by spending time with him, and the works that he wanted to do through me. After awhile, I wanted what God wanted for my life. That is something that I never would have said years ago. I thought I knew what I wanted and did whatever I could to get it. Not realizing that the one thing I needed the most was already living inside of me waiting to be set free. Even though I have made drastic changes, I am not perfect by a long shot, but I do have a greater desire to be the best representative of Christ that I can be. That leads into the last element of continuation. When you really experience the power of God in your life, I believe that there is no way that you can keep it for yourself. Sharing your faith will go far beyond threats of hell. Instead, your faith will be shown through your actions. Every day is a new mission, and full of opportunities to continue the works of Christ.

Colossians 2:6-7 says, "So then, just as you received Christ Jesus as Lord, continue to live your lives in him, rooted and built up in him, strengthened in the faith as you were taught, and overflowing with thankfulness."

To be able to encourage someone else to experience God the way that I have is nothing short of amazing. I'm no longer searching for purpose, but I am pursuing purpose with conviction. You will find that God is simply amazing if you would experience the fullness of salvation for yourself. I pray that as you continue to draw close and depend on God that you will have a similar if not better testimony than I have. I believe that the same God that was able to redeem me from my broken state and completely change my life can and will do the same for you. I can now talk about the peace of God, the love of God, and the power of God with boldness and enthusiasm. I pray that you are so empowered by this experience that you have no other choice but to share it with someone else. The butterfly is a mystical creature, produced by nothing short of a miracle. Guess what? So are you. The next time you see a butterfly, I hope that you are reminded of the metamorphosis that God desires for you. If you see a caterpillar, help it along its way. Just like you, it is on its way to becoming something great. No matter where you are, or what you have done, know that God's greatest desire is that we would all one day spread our wings and fly in his glory. It's your destiny, and it's waiting just for you. Be blessed, be you, and be free. Thank God, you were destined to fly!

The Butterfly Garden

Welcome to the garden! You are officially a part of something bigger than yourself. We are all a part of God's Kingdom, and we all need each other to carry out his will. Take a good look at your surroundings. Your garden can be made up of your job, your household, your church, your community, etc. What do you see? Are you surrounded by caterpillars and butterflies? Is there someone that is in need of new life altogether? Who can you help set free? If you are already a butterfly, be an example, as you can relate to where the caterpillar is having been there yourself. Remember that they too have the ability to fly. If you are still a caterpillar, reach out to a butterfly that you can trust and ask them to mentor you along the way, and continue to study God's word and draw close to him.

God can give you assignments to fulfill right where you are, but it is up to you to carry them out. There should always be a continual cycle of new birth and transformation happening in the body of Christ. Butterflies need to spark new life and caterpillars need to aspire to become butterflies. It is an endless cycle that we're responsible for continuing until the end of our days. If you see someone struggling in your garden, help them. If you see a wounded butterfly, find a way to lift them up. If you are the only butterfly in your garden, then you have a lot of work to do! Ask God how you can make an impact on those around you, and be sensitive to his voice. Perhaps you could treat a co-worker to lunch or make a "just because" call to a family member or loved one. Maybe you could volunteer at an organization in your community or join a ministry at your church. Whatever it is, do something to make a difference in the lives of those that are right around you. Also, it is ok to connect with other butterflies. Remember, this is not a competition, but we should be collaborating to grow God's Kingdom. Butterflies come in different sizes, colors, and patterns, and each one adds its own beauty to the world. Like so, God's children have all been given something special and unique that can be used to draw others to Christ. Surround yourself with people that can enhance your gifts, and maximize the impact that you can have on this world.

Your life matters, and the world needs you today more than ever before. As long as you're here, it's never too late to fulfill your calling. Start right where you are. The only call you'll miss is the one that you don't answer. God has placed you in your specific garden for a specific purpose. So get busy. Just because you may not be able to see who needs you, it doesn't mean that they don't exist. God will lead you to whomever he needs you to influence. That gift that you are hiding and hoarding could save somebody's life. Yes, it is that serious. When you look at the bigger picture, you will realize that everybody matters. We are all supposed to return back to God and live the life that he predestined for us. It starts with you. Your one act of obedience has the ability to impact so many people. If it didn't, God would not have given it to you. There is a certain following that you are supposed to have. There is a specific audience that you are supposed to reach. The longer you wait to do what you have been called to do, the longer those people suffer without your gift.

Understand that fulfilling your purpose has a lot to do with positioning. All you have to do is surrender to your calling, get into position, and God will work out the details. He does not need you to be perfect; he just needs you to report for duty. If you get discouraged or afraid, go spend time with God. He is the greatest comforter and supporter I know. I cannot tell you how many times I have been so unsure of what it is that He's called me to do. The only way that I could get clarity was to go to the One that gave me the assignment. Every time I did, He was there to reassure me and point me in the right direction. You have to learn to be sensitive to the Holy Spirit. It is possible to misinterpret your feelings, but do not give up. Stay close to God and he will stay close to you. Your journey will not always be easy, but you will just have to trust God and spread your wings and fly!

While you are managing your garden, remember that you still have to eat. Not only do you have to eat, but be aware of the food that you are providing to others around you. You want to keep your garden full of life. If a few weeds creep up every now and then, cut them off before they get out of control. Don't wait until they start to do damage. You could be spending your energy on something more productive rather than trying to untangle destructive weeds from your life. Continue to spend time alone with God, meditate on his word, pray, write, worship, etc. You still need to pump His power into your wings on a consistent basis in order to remain effective and pure. God did not bring you this far to leave you, nor is it time for you to leave him. You are in this thing together, and you will be until the end of your days. I hope that you enjoy your journey, and I'll meet you in the skies!

ACKNOWLEDGEMENTS

To my Lord and Savior Jesus Christ: You are an awesome wonder. No words can express my gratitude for your love and sacrifice. Without you none of this would be possible. I owe my life to you, and I pray that the world may come to know you through my works.

To my Grandma: What an awesome woman you are! I'm so blessed to have such a wonderful example of power, strength, determination, and sacrifice in my life. I love you!

To my Mom and Dad: Without you there would be no me! Through the good, bad, and the ugly, you have always been there to support me. Thank you for helping to groom me into the woman that I am today. May my accomplishments continue to make you proud. Love, the Princess.

To my brothers: Aaron, Austin, and Aiden, your sister loves you! All of you have a gift that was meant to bless the world. I pray that you will have the courage to become all that God has called you to be. You are the best little brothers a sister could ask for. I love you.

To my aunts, uncles, and cousins: I couldn't have asked for a better family. I am truly blessed to have you all in my life.

For all of the laughter, love, and the memories, I will forever be grateful. Love Always.

To my line sisters: My fellow Devastating Divas, we have come a long way! To God be the glory! I am so proud of the women that we have become. No matter how far apart we are, we share a bond that will never be broken. You all are the iron that continues to sharpen me, and you will forever hold a special place in my heart. I love you!

To my church family: God is able! You believed in me even when I didn't believe in myself. Thank you for all of your love and support through the years, and for challenging me to become the woman that God has called me to be.

To Faith Talk Toastmasters: Thank you for helping me unleash my voice! I couldn't have asked for better club members. Your support and encouragement are greatly appreciated.

NOTES

Chapter One
New Life

1. Judy Harris and Wayne Richards, *The Life Cycles of Butterflies* (North Adams, MA: Storey Publishing, 2006), 1.
2. www.enchantedlearning.com/subjects/butterfly/lifecycle/egg. Accessed 2013-02-27.
3. www.enchantedlearning.com/subjects/butterfly/lifecycle/egg. Accessed 2013-02-27.
4. Jeremiah 1:5

Chapter Four
Get Ready to Hatch

1. Judy Harris and Wayne Richards, *The Life Cycles of Butterflies* (North Adams, MA: Storey Publishing, 2006), 1.
2. www.myersbriggs.org/my-mbti-personality-type/mbti-basics/the-16-mbti-types.asp. Accessed 2013-01-12.
3. www.personalitypage.com/html/INTJ_car.html. Accessed 2013-01-12.

Chapter Five
It's Time to Eat!

1. larva.thefreedictionary.com. *The American Heritage Dictionary of the English Language.* Fourth Edition. (Houghton Mifflin Company, 2000). Accessed 2013-01-12.
2. Judy Harris and Wayne Richards, *The Life Cycles of Butterflies* (North Adams, MA: Storey Publishing, 2006), 5.
3. www.enchantedlearning.com/subjects/butterfly/lifecycle/egg. Accessed 2013-01-12.

Chapter Six
Focus on your Leaf

1. www.enchantedlearning.com/subjects/butterfly/lifecycle/larva. Accessed 2013-10-24.
2. Judy Harris and Wayne Richards, *The Life Cycles of Butterflies* (North Adams, MA: Storey Publishing, 2006), 5.

Chapter Seven
The Signs of Growth

1. Judy Harris and Wayne Richards, *The Life Cycles of Butterflies* (North Adams, MA: Storey Publishing, 2006), 5.
2. Judy Harris and Wayne Richards, *The Life Cycles of Butterflies* (North Adams, MA: Storey Publishing, 2006), 5.

Chapter Eight
Caterpillars Can't Fly

1. Hebrews 11:6

Chapter Nine
Hanging on by a Thread

1. Judy Harris and Wayne Richards, *The Life Cycles of Butterflies* (North Adams, MA: Storey Publishing, 2006), 8.
2. Judy Harris and Wayne Richards, *The Life Cycles of Butterflies* (North Adams, MA: Storey Publishing, 2006), 8.
3. Judy Harris and Wayne Richards, *The Life Cycles of Butterflies* (North Adams, MA: Storey Publishing, 2006), 9.

Chapter Ten
All Wrapped Up

1. Judy Harris and Wayne Richards, *The Life Cycles of Butterflies* (North Adams, MA: Storey Publishing, 2006), 9.
2. www.enchantedlearning.com/subjects/butterfly/lifecycle/pupa. Accessed 2013-02-03.
3. Matthew 22:37-39
4. Job 1:21

5. Judy Harris and Wayne Richards, *The Life Cycles of Butterflies* (North Adams, MA: Storey Publishing, 2006), 8.

6. Romans 8:1

Chapter Eleven

The Ultimate Surrender

1. Judy Harris and Wayne Richards, *The Life Cycles of Butterflies* (North Adams, MA: Storey Publishing, 2006), 9.

Chapter Twelve

Be Transformed!

1. Judy Harris and Wayne Richards, *The Life Cycles of Butterflies* (North Adams, MA: Storey Publishing, 2006), 11.

2. Judy Harris and Wayne Richards, *The Life Cycles of Butterflies* (North Adams, MA: Storey Publishing, 2006), 11.

3. Judy Harris and Wayne Richards, *The Life Cycles of Butterflies* (North Adams, MA: Storey Publishing, 2006), 11.

Chapter Fourteen

Just Fly

1. Judy Harris and Wayne Richards, *The Life Cycles of Butterflies* (North Adams, MA: Storey Publishing, 2006), 12.

Chapter Fifteen

Don't Lose Sight of the Ground

1. Judy Harris and Wayne Richards, *The Life Cycles of Butterflies* (North Adams, MA: Storey Publishing, 2006), 15.
2. Judy Harris and Wayne Richards, *The Life Cycles of Butterflies* (North Adams, MA: Storey Publishing, 2006), 15.